Early

MW00616199

For Mary Yuan
And Where Is Home?

"*Where is Home* is beautiful, poignant, and real, a stunning memoir that provides an unflinching look at family post-divorce. Mary Yuan brilliantly allows her reader to see the remaking of a life.

    – Christine Ristaino, Professor at Emory University, Award-winning Author of *All the Silent Spaces*

"I am very impressed with what Mary is doing! Her subject matter 'home' resonates with me because I lived overseas for 14 years and my family includes several cultures. Whatever she puts her mind to is bound to be a success and this book is one of her stunning endeavors."

    – Rajiv Kapoor, Investor at Chai Angels

"This heartwarming coming-of-age memoir is an important reminder that 'home' can take on a variety of forms and shapes, the foundation of which is compassion and kindness."

    – Thamina Stoll, Account Director at LinkedIn

"A must-read for anyone who has ever wondered 'Where is home?' Mary's natural writing flair immerses you into her world. Having lived abroad 1/3 of my life, I instantly connected with Mary. She truly wants all the people around the world who feel that they don't belong to connect with each other. Let's unite!"   **– Rania Svoronou, Design Director at IBM iX**

"Through stories of her solo travels abroad, Yuan explores the inner strength, love, and hope that it takes to discover that belonging starts from within."

    – Belinda Lei, Yale School of Management MBA, Software Engineer at Citi

"If you have ever wondered how to heal and create a sense of belonging when feeling uprooted or lost, Yuan's book will guide you and help you power through some of the most challenging times in your life."

    – Vanessa Millones, Georgetown MBA, Obama White House Alumna

"As Mary's intimate storytelling flings us through her soaring highs and crushing lows, we find ourselves both laughing and crying in her personal moments. But most importantly, as much as *Where is Home?* teaches us about Mary, it teaches us more about ourselves and our own journeys."

    – Ryan Lee, Sr. Data Analyst at The Walt Disney Company

"A beautiful memoir woven together with solo traveling and deep reckoning. Yuan uses her own experiences as a jumping off point to redefine what home means to each of us. A must-read for the most challenging times in your life."

– Charlene Wang, Associate Product Manager at Google

"Being vulnerable is difficult, but it's a foundational part of life. Mary Yuan leads by example and makes vulnerability look easy by sharing her life with the world. *Where Is Home?* shows what it means to be open to change, growth, and life."

– Michelle Zhao, Associate at Boston Consulting Group

"Mary Yuan has woven a vibrant narrative tapestry, and has allowed us to join her on what I imagine has been a painstaking rollercoaster of a journey. With this book, she has enabled us to deeply contemplate the meaning of 'home,' and what it means to each one of us."

– Kiran Sundar, SAP Consultant at EY

"Mary's ability to bring readers into not only her world but have them see their own lives through new lenses is both inspiring and comforting. *Where is Home?* is a must-read that reminds us of who we truly are and gives us the hope, wisdom, and perspective we need to rediscover home within ourselves."   *– Natanya Bravo, Founder of The Bravo Life*

"*Where Is Home?* shares a vulnerable and uplifting story of Mary Yuan's soul-searching journey to heal childhood trauma through solo travel. Mary's inspiring story teaches readers how Mary found hope, connection, and joy despite challenging circumstances."

– Jaclyn DiGregorio, Best-selling Author, Motivational Speaker and Life Coach

"A deeply moving and empowering memoir filled with life's wisdoms that transcend age, cultural background, or gender. Yuan invites us to her journey to find home, and inspires us to find our own sense of belonging."

– Kevin Zhen, Founder and CEO of ZhenEd LLC

"Mary's relentless spirit, perseverance and unparalleled confidence in *Where is Home?* transcends the pages of her book to inspire readers to cherish moments on our life's journey as opportunities to rediscover ourselves."

– Nicole Spindler, HR Analyst at BNY Mellon

WHERE IS HOME?

WHERE IS HOME?

A TRAVEL MEMOIR OF BELONGING, HEALING, AND IDENTITY

MARY YUAN

(袁梦瑶, MY CHINESE NAME MEANS
"TO REALIZE MY FARAWAY DREAMS")

NEW DEGREE PRESS

WHERE IS HOME?
A Travel Memoir of Belonging, Healing, and Identity

ISBN   978-1-63676-605-8 *Paperback*
           978-1-63676-266-1 *Kindle Ebook*
           978-1-63676-267-8 *Ebook*

To my mom, who has taught me the strength of vulnerability and the capacity to love; and to my grandma, who always reminds me to stay true to my cultural identity. To my dad, who loves me in a way no one else can in this world.

To all the adult children of divorce, solo travelers, expats, and anyone who yearns to find home and belonging, know that you are not alone.

I am here to listen and share my story with you.

TABLE OF CONTENTS

———

"I think that when you invite people to your home, you invite them to yourself."

—OPRAH WINFREY

AUTHOR'S NOTES

Where is home for me if my parents are divorced? How can I find home again after feeling lost and uprooted?

My memoir takes you on my solo travels to find home after my parents' divorce. It takes you on my journey of rebuilding trust and happiness as a twenty-two-year-old female solo traveler. On many occasions, I felt at home with locals in the places to which I traveled. Over time, those precious and inspiring moments propelled me to reconnect with my broken family, rebuild my own home, and write this book to empower you.

My family is only one example among the broken households in which many children are living. Almost 40–50 percent of all marriages in the US will end in divorce.[1] That number is more staggering in European countries such as Belgium, where the divorce rate is around 60–70 percent.[2]

The startling global divorce rate almost desensitizes us in terms of getting a divorce or experiencing our parents' divorce. Many professors and friends encouraged me to "let it go and move on," "go home to your parents," or "get counseling." They spoke as if they knew those options would be effective, or even feasible, in helping me through my difficult time. Though I believe they had good intentions, their suggestions simply

---

1 "Marriage and Divorce," American Psychological Association, accessed October 4, 2020.

2 "Divorce Rate by Country: The World's 10 Most and Least Divorced Nations," *United Lawyers* (blog), September 29, 2017, accessed October 8, 2020.

downplayed the complexity of a disruptive trauma and the personal healing process that comes after it.

The post-trauma stage should not be rushed, and one should not try to "quickly get it over with." How can you let go of your family who used to be your rock and safe haven? How can you go home to your parents when it is cut in half?

Usually, home is where we turn to when we need to let down our deepest fears or most cutting pain. Home is where we feel safe and anchor our hearts. However, what if that place has turned into the source of insecurity and pain?

When I realized my family was no longer a source of support I could depend on, I chose to break away and travel solo to release my grief and rediscover myself.

Traveling is familiar to me because I have studied abroad for almost a third of my life. I am one of the 272 million people around the world who live in a country other than where they were born.[3] In the past, my courage to constantly take risks and explore faraway lands was based on the security I felt from my home. After my parents' divorce, rebuilding home was especially crucial to me.

I had the strong urge to break away as far as possible from the painful reality that I no longer had a complete family. It would be easy and convenient for me to look away, cutting myself off from my dad, who caused my family so much pain. However, the most rewarding process for me was to find home again after traveling solo. I realized traveling loses its essence if, at the end of the day, there is no home to return to.

---

3   Charlotte Edmond, "Global Migration, by the Numbers: Who Migrates, Where They Go and Why," *World Economic Forum*, January 10, 2020, accessed October 4, 2020.

The beauty of having a broken home is that it pushes you to dive deep into the meaning of home and try to find a way to rebuild it. The purpose of healing is not to move on as fast as you can or to bury the pain ruthlessly. Healing starts the moment you embrace your new reality and try to actively rebuild the broken link of trust, happiness, and home. When you finally find your way out of the pain and trauma, the awful memories of the past can be laid to rest.

When I had no option to go back to the home I used to have, instead of seeking security, I embarked on a solo journey that brought new perspectives to my old questions.

I believe the answers to your questions are within you. I believe in your power of healing your wound with your own hands. I believe home can be rebuilt. I also believe in soul searching, connecting with people you've never met, and finding your home through solo traveling. Most importantly, I believe home is more than where you were, but where you are and where you are going.

My memoir is for you if life threw a big trauma at you and you are struggling to cope. If you have been cheated by your family, friends, or significant other, this book encourages you to consider giving them a second chance. This is also for you if you are a solo traveler who is hesitant to take the first step toward your dream adventures. You will resonate with my story if you are living away from the place you were born, and you want to reconnect with your roots while building kinship. If you are exploring the meaning of trust, love, happiness, traveling, home, and even yourself, this memoir is for you.

Before we start our journey to find home, let us first take a moment and ask ourselves: Where is home?

PART 1

LOST MY HOME

"Nothing could cut me deeper than hearing about my parents' divorce—and worse, the reason."

CHAPTER 1

Falling Into the Abyss

———

Atlanta, October 2016. The winds were howling on a dark and stormy day. As the bell rang, the last Philosophy lecture ended in a flurry of chatter and rapid packing. Chipper college sophomores were forced into the brutal freeze and appalling gloom to return to their dorms. I was pushed outside by a current of crowds.

As I sped to my dorm, the wind was cutting my face so painfully that tears were gathering in the corners of my eyes. After what felt like an eternity, I stumbled into the warmth and comfort of my dorm. I dropped the heavy backpack from my shoulders and collapsed onto my bean bag.

Soon, I heard my phone ring. I picked up the WeChat video call from Beijing, the other side of the Pacific Ocean.

"妈妈! (Mama!)" I was so excited to see my mom again after a month of busy schoolwork. Last time, we chatted about possible family vacation plans during my winter break.

"瑶瑶, 这么久也没跟妈妈联系! (You've not reached out for a while... you have no idea how much I miss you...)" Mom put on a smile, but I could see her nose was red and tears were on the brink of falling from her eyes.

"妈, 怎么啦? (Mom, how are you?)" I thought Mom missed me so much that she could not control her emotions.

"我得告诉你件事儿。(I need to tell you something...)" Mom responded in a heavy tone.

"嗯? (...yes?)" My heart was racing, and my head was filled with all sorts of anxious speculations.

Mom usually didn't sound this sullen; I could sense from all the complicated emotions written on her face that it was more than her desperately missing me. Fear loomed in my mind as I waited for the words to come out of her mouth.

"你爸出轨啦, 还有个小孩儿。(Your dad... he cheated... and... a baby...)" Mom was sobbing, "我们办离婚了。(...he and I are divorced.)"

I dropped my phone on the floor, jaw wide open but unable to speak a word. Mom's words shattered my identity into pieces, and all the memories of my family burst into flames. I could not believe what she had just said. I refused to surrender to the earth-shattering news.

This news could not be true. Dad would not hurt my mom like that. Dad could not hurt me like this. He would never... he promised the world to this family and he would never let me down. He is so strong and would always protect... He always told me to be honest, especially to the ones I love... but he... All of these thoughts were spinning faster and faster in my head, like a tornado, and it was all so crushing that I felt lightheaded and saw stars before my eyes. I did not know what to think, what to feel, not to mention what to say.

"喂？你还在听吗？ (Hello? Are you still there?)" Mom's voice came from my phone.

I felt like I was suffocating. It was killing me to hear her voice and see her pain. I could not take it anymore. I picked up the phone from the floor and threw it across the room. It banged against the wall and died.

"*Why?*" I screamed and burst out into a loud and heart-wrenching cry, "*Why? Why? How could...*" I picked up anything within my reach and broke the items into pieces. I tore apart the things I once cherished—the photos of me and my parents, my essays about love and trust, and my past birthday gifts from my dad. Watching those things torn and scattered on the floor was still not enough. I trampled the debris violently, questioning why they existed in the first place. In mere seconds, I turned into a frantic beast.

Why did I only find out about my parents' divorce after it happened? They had fights occasionally, but I did not imagine my dad would betray my mom. I found myself in a particularly difficult situation also because parents don't get divorced in my culture, or, at least, it is taboo. Divorced households are considered failures, and there is no doubt that people will talk. "看，她父母离异啦。唉，出轨的那点儿事！ (Look, her parents are divorced. Sigh, adultery!)" People outside of the family would judge, and even my own relatives probably spoke about it behind my back.

With only my pajamas on, I stormed out of my room and ran into the overwhelming cold and dangerously dark night.

I kept running and screaming into the darkness. Fury. Sadness. Hatred. Indignation. Pain. They all occupied my body, eating up my beliefs, my memories, and my heart. At that moment, the cutting pain of the wind on my face and in my eyes felt like nothing. Nothing could cut me deeper than hearing about my parents' divorce—and worse, the reason for it.

I felt unloved, lost, wrenched, torn, and doomed—doomed to be miserable for God knows how long. I felt so disgusted and hopeless in the face of a reality in my life that was out of my control. It was like being defeated in a battle for which I did not ask.

All the vibrant and happy memories of my parents and I suddenly became black and white. Our family vacations abroad and the holidays we spent together felt like lies. I had never felt so out of touch with happiness, security, and my identity. Family became a broken promise and a distant past. All the beautiful stories about love, trust, and commitment started to sound like bullshit to me.

Before that night, whenever I was in pain, or whenever I needed to talk to someone but knew no one else would understand, I could turn to my family. The call with my mom that night changed everything—that safe haven where I felt the safest and most loved was destroyed. I never thought that one day I would hate my dad so much. His strong, responsible, and dependable image in my heart became a joke.

I ran until I could no longer catch my breath. Finally, I fell on the grass at the quad and let myself lie there, engulfed by the chilly night. I let my fears creep into my psyche, killing whatever ounce of joy was left in me. I was paralyzed but still tried to call to the murky sky for an answer. All I received was silence—the kind that is quiet and deadly. For a while, I became the deadly silence—I could not think; I could not feel; I could not speak.

Exhausted and emotionally drained, I fell asleep in that 10°F temperature with the howling wind all around me.

However, deep down in my heart, no matter how much bliss bled out of it or how many pieces it was torn into, my heart was still longing for somewhere warm, somewhere nothing bad could happen, somewhere that could feel like home.

When I woke up again, the watch on my right wrist told me it was 1:00 a.m. I dragged myself back to the little space of my dorm and stared at the ceiling until I fell asleep. Shattered gifts and torn photos quietly lay on the floor. No one was around with whom I could share my grief. Even if my best friends were there by my side, they would not understand the heavy and gut-wrenching new reality I was dealing with. Plus, I wouldn't want to bring up my parents' divorce in a casual conversation with my girlfriends on a Friday night. I was all alone.

I felt myself falling into this abyss. Just falling with no pain, no feelings, and no sense of time. No more tears to cry.

CHAPTER 2

Birthday Long-Life Noodles and Spring Festival Dumplings

About one month after my mom broke the heart-wrenching news about the divorce, there I was, lying on my bed, tightly holding my soft comforter. Usually, home was the place I returned to whenever I needed a safe haven, but now it was broken and far away. So the only place I could seek any form of comfort and security was my bed. Nothing painful could happen here.

My heart seemed to ache more each day.

When happiness did not present itself in front of me, I felt inclined to pursue it, even if it was just pieces of memories that no longer existed as reality. I missed several things about my family, including those carefree and adventurous family vacations to faraway destinations, all of which now felt like a distant memory. But most of all, I missed the collection of little moments that happen every day; those touch the softest spot in my heart.

A thread of mystical moonlight illuminated my dusty memories, bringing me back to my third birthday.

It was a sunny mid-spring Friday. My height just reached a bit above the arm of the couch in my living room. Mom always said—and still says—my birthday matches my personality perfectly. My birthday, April 14, is unarguably the peak of spring, when locals swim in the sweet flower seas and kites soar freely in the baby blue sky.

During the most beautiful season of the year, everything is awakened by the energy of birth, growth, and renewal.

Spring in Beijing is blissful in the most unique sense and vibrant in the best possible way. One could casually take a stroll in the Summer Palace and find their cheeks kissed by the soft and fragrant breeze by the lake. The gazebos, bridges, and palaces silently share their glorious stories that have been told for thousands of years, taking you back to an ancient empire. Looking across the mirror-like surface, you might discover a fleet of fluffy newborn ducklings or some boats embellishing the calm watercolor scenery. Many people come out to soak up the warm spring sun after battling through the brutally freezing winter.

On my special day, Mommy and Daddy freed themselves from work and took a whole day off to make me the happiest and luckiest birthday girl in the world. They took me to the park, and we relished in the warmth and colors that spring had to offer. We walked along the serpentine path covered by a peach blossom petal carpet. Mom held my right hand

and Dad grabbed my left. The three of us fit perfectly in the beautiful picture of the magical springtime.

Dad always knew how to amuse my curious heart, so he brought a bag of bread flakes for me to feed the chirping birds on the trees and the packs of ducklings and goslings floating in the water. Sporadically, Dad picked me up from the ground by surprise and put me on his wide and firm shoulder so I could overlook the sweeping view. On his shoulders, I no longer felt like a small three-year-old who always thought the world was so big. Instead, I felt like an almighty queen, majestically ruling my kingdom with a dazzling crown on my head. Dad made me feel like I could take on the world.

Mom's devotion to me was detailed and subtle. She dressed me up like a princess: a diamond tiara on my head with fresh handpicked pink peach blossoms, my hair carefully braided, a brand-new baby pink tulle fairy dress, and a pair of red sparkling low-heel shoes. Wherever I pranced around, people stopped and asked, "这小天使是谁呀? (Who is this gorgeous angel?)"

After we enjoyed ourselves in the park, Mom and Dad took me back home. I could never imagine that one day I would lose all the precious time we spent together.

As I glanced at the pile of torn photos and smashed picture frames on the floor where I left them, I felt like everything I knew and loved was gone. I had lost it all. I sunk deeper into my bed and once again dreamed up happiness within my mind.

On the sun-soaked balcony, Dad and I were building a temple and a plane using wooden model kits, and Mom was busy preparing Long-Life Noodles for me in the kitchen. 长寿面 *Long-Life Noodles* play a significant role during birthdays in Chinese culture. They derive their name from the specially handmade noodle that is long enough to fill up an entire bowl, uncut. The lengthy noodle connotes the best birthday wish that one lives as long as the noodle. The beautiful tradition aside, Mom's Long-Life Noodles are not like any other because they simply taste the best!

The magic starts with the beef tendon broth cooked with spinach for an hour. Mom always reminded me that every good dish starts with a solid base, a key lesson applicable to many things in life. Then the critical, and perhaps the most difficult, part is stretching the super long noodle without breaking it. What seems to be an impossible task became a delightful art performance in Mom's hands. Her slim fingers swiftly and adeptly rotated and rolled the noodle against the wooden cutting board, stretching it longer with every twist. It took about half an hour to mold the perfect long-life noodle without breaking it at any point. By the time Mom tossed the noodle into the broth, I could see sweat dripping down from her forehead, but her face seemed relaxed and a soft smile lingered on her lips.

While waiting for the noodles to be ready, Dad and I had a great time together. Dad always treated me like his son and said he wanted me to be healthy and sturdy like a boy. Our bonding time was usually spent building some complex wooden models that boys are often crazy about. I had so much fun building stuff with Dad because it made me feel like we were partners in crime, trying to crack a challenging yet exciting puzzle together. Whenever Dad was around, I always felt that nothing is impossible, and I believed in myself a bit more.

Mom came out with two bowls of steamy noodles that filled the room with the rich aroma of broth. She placed the bigger bowl in front of me and the other one in front of Dad. Mom always put everyone else first, and sometimes I have to remind her to think of herself.

"生日快乐! 瑶瑶今天就三岁啦! (Happy birthday! Can't believe our dear Yaoyao is turning three years old today!)" Mom and Dad also could not contain their excitement as they clapped and then pinched my cheeks.

Though at times off-key, Mom and Dad sang the birthday song to me fondly, and I could see the emotion in their teary eyes as they finished with, "瑶瑶长得真快! (Yaoyao is growing so fast!)"

We sat together around our dinner table, savoring Mom's delicious noodles and her love cooked into the meal.

In my dark, prison-like dorm room, with old, stale cafeteria noodles in a crusty bowl on my desk, my eyes finally closed, my mind drifting away to dreamland.

I dreamed of home.

I pushed myself up from my bed and tiptoed into the living room. My jaw dropped when I saw the red lanterns, Chinese knots, and paper cuttings of tigers and dragons decorating every corner of the room. I gasped and realized it was the day of the Spring Festival, one of the most important Chinese holidays.

When I still had a complete loving family, the Spring Festival was my favorite time of the year. The start date of the festivities follows the lunar calendar, so it varies depending on the year. Sometimes it happens around mid or late January, and other times it does not start until mid-February.

Regardless of the date, it occurs during the bone-chilling winter. Often, people have to push through the howling wind and harsh snowstorms to make it home. The determination to be home on time regardless of the testing weather speaks to the significance of reunion in the hearts of billions of Chinese people.

Families still practice many traditions to this day. People begin preparing a few weeks before the start date of the Spring Festival. Like many families, my parents and grandma took me to different markets to secure the most exquisite and one-of-a-kind decorations before anyone else could buy them. We were dazzled by numerous lanterns and paper arts. We enjoyed the little competition because the shopping process bound us together as a team against the rest of the families.

When we returned home with bags of goodies, Mom and I took charge of decorating our whole house. Mom had the otherworldly power to beautify our home with her great sense of interior design. She is the person who makes home a place where I feel deeply connected. I followed her like a little duckling around the house to give her a helping hand if she needed to hang the lanterns and knots by the windows or stick the paper arts on the walls. The decorating process normally takes hours, and by the end of it, every corner of the house has something red-colored, which means good luck in Chinese culture.

Even now that I am an adult, when it is close to the Spring Festival, I yearn to follow Mom like a duckling and run around the house together, embellishing everything in red, which also happens to be my favorite color.

On the evening before the festival, Grandma, Mom, and I gathered around in the kitchen to make 饺子 *Jiaozi*, which are Chinese dumplings. It is an art Grandma passed along to me.

"看? (See?)" Grandma said. "用筷子把馅儿压紧，把皮儿填满。 (Use your chopsticks to stuff as much filling as possible in one wrapper.)"

Grandma always showed me how to make big dumplings so they stood firmly on the cutting board. She closed up the wrapper with her fingers, aptly squeezing the top to form a ruffled crown around the edge. When making dumplings, Grandma became a creative magician who could turn plain dumplings into the shapes of a bunny, lotus, sunflower, or a little mouse. Grandma is also a nutrition expert. Even in making the fillings for the dumplings, she made sure there were enough veggies to go with some hints of meat. Her favorite combo is cabbage and winter radish paired with sea bass. I always stood next to her and looked at the magic in her hands in awe. While more and more dumplings came to life in her hands, a proud grin surfaced on her face and warmed my heart, reminding me of how lucky I am to have a loving family.

As a family tradition, we randomly stuffed a select few dumplings with a peanut or a coin, so that whoever discovers those were the lucky ones. Little games like that made the family dinner even more fun and exciting because everyone raced to eat as many dumplings as possible in hope of getting the right ones. The steamy dumplings warmed up the dining room the four of us shared, in stark contrast against the brutal cold outside.

Isn't this what home is? The place where you share warmth with your family against the cold world outside?

In my sleep, as I dreamed about the cold outside my family home during the Spring Festival and felt the cold in my lonely dorm room, I shivered and pulled the blanket up closer to my face.

After dinner, it was time to watch the Spring Festival gala. My family gathered in front of the TV, laughed at the comedies, and marveled at the dragon dancers. Typically, it runs throughout the night until dawn because it is a tradition that everyone stays up to greet the new year. It would have been impossible to sleep even if I had tried because families celebrate with incessant, thunderous fireworks too stunning to miss. Usually, the prime time to watch fireworks is right after the gala, and the grand finale can last until 4:00 a.m.

Dad purchased fireworks in bulk so he could light them up to present a spectacular fireworks show for the whole family. I remember feeling that lighting the fireworks was a dangerous task, but Dad's swift motions made it seemed like a piece of cake. His bravery is the foundation of my pride in my family and inspires me not to be afraid of risks.

Fireworks have a special meaning during the Chinese New Year because they are believed to have the power to blow up all the bad luck (年 Nian, the symbol of bad luck, is a monster who haunts families at the year's end, according to Chinese folklore) in the past year so the new year can bring joy and fortune. The vibrant colors coupled with the blasting sound syncopated with my heartbeats. Enjoying the stunning fireworks that light up the dark sky with my family marked the climax of the night.

Many clusters of colors blasted in the sky, but none could ever compare with the ones Dad lit up because they belonged to my family.

When we were exhausted from cheering for the fireworks in the snow, we returned to our warm house. Sometimes we stayed at Grandma's place, and I watched Mom, Dad, and Grandma playing cards. Other times, we visited Dad's side of the family. His three older brothers and their families would get together to play 麻将 *Mahjong*. I did not know a thing about the rules of *Mahjong*, but I was so delighted to watch a big family engaged with their fun game and banters by the table. Seeing them happy was all that mattered to me.

I woke up with a start, as if fireworks had gone off in my college dorm room. I tried to look around in the darkness, but there was nothing. I felt empty and completely alone. The sound of the fireworks blasting and people cheering were all just a dream.

Everything felt so real.

My dreams and memories were convincingly vivid. I could still feel my parents' embrace when I jumped into their arms as they sang "Happy Birthday!" I could still feel the warmth of their hands holding mine while we were strolling in the flower seas in springtime. I could still feel the taste of Mom's Long-Life Noodles and Grandma's dumplings.

Now that I am on the other side of the world, I often miss those times when everyone gathered in a big house to celebrate, have fun, and give each other warm wishes. Because of my parents' divorce, gathering all family members in one place could never happen again.

PART 2

THE HOME I HAD

"Something is cherished even more once
it is taken away."

CHAPTER 3

Traveling the World With My Home

———

"Solo traveling is my way of challenging myself to explore the unknown," Dad used to tell me in Mandarin.

Because of Dad, holidays were the best time of the year for my family. When we traveled, he often told me the story of how he learned to love traveling. Dad did not grow up in a loving family, so he became defiantly independent. When his parents did not support his going to college, Dad flew away from his home to Japan and completed his undergraduate studies there. He had to work three part-time jobs to pay his college tuition, and completing his degree was a proud triumph for him. Since then, he has never stopped stepping foot on foreign lands.

He also shared with me that solo traveling was sometimes a lonely venture. Dad made sure I never felt lonely while traveling because by traveling as a family, we avoided the quagmire of solitude. At the end of our adventures, wherever we were, we had our home with us—my home was wherever my parents and I were together.

Dad took Mom and I to Malaysia when I was three. It was 2000, a year that feels so distant now. I was too young to remember the names of the places we had been to, but I do recall some moments that shine like diamonds through the dust of time.

It might have been the first time I was on a plane. Right before the plane took off, my muscles started to tense up. My arms gripped the handles of my seat, and I leaned back with my legs stretched out, as if I was trying to counterbalance the unpleasant angle of elevation. Mom sat on my right side, Dad on the left. They both chuckled when they saw my stiff and miserable posture. "放松！试着享受。(Relax! Try to enjoy it.)" Dad put his hand on mine. The plane's engine was roaring loud, and my ears popped as we rose. Once we were high up in the sky, I felt lifted like a bird gliding among the clouds. "See? Told you. Have to enjoy it." Dad gave me a sly grin.

My family spent almost three weeks in Malaysia. I have vague memories of the resort where we stayed, and we were on the beach or on the boat most of the time. The beachfront resort connected to the lush green foliage of the island. An artificial waterfall poured water into an infinity pool.

One evening, when the sun painted the clouds pink and vermilion, Dad took me to the pool and said he would teach me how to swim. Mom watched us from an ivory-curtained cabana by the pool. First, Dad flopped into the pool and created a huge splash of water, shrieking as he dived in. It looked crazy fun, so I started pacing impatiently by the pool. At first, I could not locate Dad because he dove into the water without resurfacing for a while. Then suddenly, his head popped up right in front of me.

"Come! I'm going to hold you in my arms and you will just float." Dad gestured for me to jump into the pool as well.

However, as a three-year-old, I was terrified of the water. I did not even like washing my face that much because I was not a fan of breathing with my mouth. Dad kept splashing water at me and said he would not stop until I got into the pool. So I took a deep breath and milked my courage right before I took a big leap into the seemingly bottomless water.

When I dove in, my instinct propelled my body upward so that I could inhale some air again. My eyes were tightly shut, resisting any drop of water from irritating my eyeballs. There were no Dad's arms to be found. I started treading water harder to keep my head above the water.

Dad was a couple of feet away, watching me the whole time. I started splashing water at him because I felt scared and betrayed. "You promised to catch me!" I screamed at Dad furiously. I turned around and saw Mom's face, stunned. What made me even more upset was that Dad started laughing. "Okay okay! I am simply glad that you figured it out all by yourself." Dad tried to dodge the water splashes while telling me how proud he was.

For the rest of the pool time, Dad helped me adjust a few postures while swimming. But most of the time, we just enjoyed ourselves in the pool. Dad sometimes lifted me high in the air with his strong arms and then dropped me into the water. I had asked him to because I no longer felt afraid of water. Dad swam around like a fish, whereas I was trying hard to mimic him.

When we finally came out of the pool, Mom bumped Dad's arm and blamed him for being too careless, "What if she drowned? You were too far away from her to help her. She's only three."

"That's how she impressed me, by figuring out how to float on her own!" Dad still could not help smiling. "That's my daughter." He then patted me on the back.

For dinner, we went to a local restaurant. I can't recall what we ate, but Dad never let me forget one highlight. We were accompanied by other travelers, who joined us. When the servers presented the swarm of delicacies on the dinner table, before anyone reacted, I jumped and collected a few dishes and put them right next to Dad.

"This is reserved for my dad!" I hollered and protected the food from anyone else with my arms.

Everyone at the table burst into laughter and complimented me on how adorable I was. "I'm jealous that you have such a good daughter!" One gentleman sitting across the table told my parents.

Many years later, whenever he was dining with friends, Dad still bragged about how lucky he was to have such a loving daughter at the dinner table.

***

In 2004, I turned seven years old, and it was also the first time I traveled solo. My choir had a performance in Bangkok, but I could not arrive at the same time as my peers, as I was finishing up a final exam.

When Mom came to pick me up from the exam room to take me to the airport, I ran out of the building and hopped into the car.

"I've got your luggage. It's in the trunk. And your dad put a Leica camera in your backpack. He reminds you not to forget to capture the moments. Most of all, be safe!" Mom sped the car through the traffic, full speed toward the airport.

"Are you guys not coming with me?" I was not aware that I was going to fly to Thailand on my own.

"Yes, honey. Dad is out of town for business, and I have so much at hand to do too. Besides, Dad and I wanted to challenge you to be brave and see if you could take care of yourself," Mom said with confidence.

"Wow, okay. How exciting!" I clapped my hands. Though I was seven, I was not at all scared of the idea of traveling solo. Instead, it was thrilling. Dad's independent spirit inspired me to become a kindred adventurer.

At the airport, Mom and I pushed our way through the bustling crowds. We found our way to the airline check-in desk.

"Ma'am, are you traveling with the kid?" the stewardess kindly asked Mom.

"No. Is there any way to make sure she gets to Bangkok safely?" Mom's voice started to shake. I could only imagine how much she was worried about me, though she appeared to be confident for my sake.

"Okay... in that case, we will get a designated flight attendant to escort your daughter at all times. That's no problem." She gave my mom a reassuring smile.

I had only twenty minutes until my flight took off. A tall and kind lady in her late twenties walked toward me and said, "Hello, doll, I'm going to fly with you to Bangkok." Mom seemed content with the lady who would take care of me.

The flight attendant wore a chic uniform and looked charmingly handsome. She leaned over and put a bright yellow sign on my neck. Back then, I had no clue what it said, but later mom told me it allowed me to pass through security in no time.

The flight attendant seated me at A1, a window seat in first class. When I buckled myself up and looked out the window, I felt a surge of joyful anticipation. It was getting more real by the minute that I would fly to Bangkok and join my choir, all by myself.

When the plane started to take off, Dad's reminder came back to me, "Relax! Enjoy it." Over the next five hours, I alternated between reading and gazing out of the window to watch clouds floating by. When I was enjoying my flight, I thought about the Leica camera Mom mentioned. I reached into my backpack and pulled out the camera. When I held it in my hand, it felt like Dad was right next to me, ready to start this adventure together.

I took a couple of photos of the clouds and asked the flight attendant to take a photo of me. It felt like a celebration of me as a first-time solo traveler, as a fierce seven-year-old girl.

When I landed in Bangkok safely, I parted with the flight attendant. Instantly, I felt anxious again. As I looked around, I saw signs in languages I could not understand. People much taller than me hustled around and made me feel lost and dizzy. My instinct pushed me toward a taxi. I hopped in and showed the driver the address sent to me. After a few minutes, I joined my choir. My peers cheered for my bravery and success in finding them.

It was utterly surreal to me that I made it. Even to this day, when I travel alone and occasionally find myself feeling nervous, I remind myself how fearless I was as a seven-year-old.

During my time in Thailand with my choir, I took many photos with Dad's Leica camera. Whenever I felt homesick, the camera reminded me of Dad. It almost felt like he was right there with me when I was exploring the jungles in the forest, or holding a baby alligator in my hand later in my solo travels as an adult. The camera was a piece of home for me that I carried everywhere. Though at times I felt alone and lost, my dad's camera reminded me that there was always a home waiting for me to return to.

***

One year later, my family took a two-month vacation in Australia. As usual, Dad carried his camera to take photos of me throughout our travels.

Though I didn't really enjoy it when he demanded that I pose exactly as he told me to, I complied most of the time. I did not realize it was a blessing to have a dad who hated to miss even the smallest moment.

We traveled to the desert, picnicked with couples on the lawn, saw baby penguins flop into the ocean to swim for the first time, and visited most of the major landmarks. Dad always pushed me to interact with the locals. Though it did not feel natural to me to speak with total strangers in a foreign language, he still pushed me. I did not have a choice.

One of the people who really wanted to chat with me was the private driver who drove us around. At that point, my English was, at most, elementary school level. I tried to chat with the driver using the basics. He seemed to be very enthusiastic about chatting with me. However, the more we talked, the less I could understand, and at a certain point, I became completely speechless. Though I wanted to respond to his hospitality, I was simply unable to. My words ran out. I finally gave up after five minutes of not speaking a word and nodding my head cluelessly. I felt embarrassed because I was on the spot, with my parents standing next to me and a crowd gathering around me and the driver. I could not endure the torture anymore, and I could feel tears well up in my eyes.

I ran away abruptly toward Mom. She wrapped me in her arms, and said, "It's okay. You did great."

Running out of words while trying to chat with that driver planted a seed in my head to learn English more diligently. I promised myself I'd get to a point where language would no longer be a barrier to expressing myself and connecting with people.

Years later, I could not help but look back at all the beautiful memories I shared with my parents while we were traveling the world together. No matter where we were, Dad always enthusiastically captured the moments of me and my mom. Of course, now Mom keeps stacks of albums that include photos Dad took of me during our family vacations. Though some were torn into pieces when I first heard about my dad's betrayal of my family, Mom's remaining photos helped me keep the memories alive.

When I returned to Thailand and Indonesia on my own while I traveled solo, the mango rice still tasted the same, and the white sand beach still looked pristine stretching out into a serene cove. However, everything about my family had changed. I no longer had a home waiting for me while I traveled the world.

CHAPTER 4

Two Months in the Hospital

———

On the evening of September 6, 2009, when I was twelve years old, I was in bed with a fever for days. According to the thermometer, my temperature peaked at an alarming 39°C (102°F). Mom took me to the hospital that day because my body was burning so badly that I started to slur words incoherently.

Around me, doctors were all suited up in pale white gowns with their white masks and gloves on. In the emergency room, I was shocked to see some patients whose faces were barely recognizable with white bandages wrapped around their heads. They looked like zombies except their blood was still oozing out, painting the bandages in sharp red. It was like being trapped in a maze inside a horror movie. Fear was eating everyone alive, and it fueled me with the impulse to run away—except there was nowhere to go.

"你叫什么名字? (What's your name?)" Dr. Li looked at me and asked while typing information into his computer.

"袁梦瑶。(Yuan Mengyao,)" I said, coughing mid-speech.

"有什么症状？(Could you describe your symptoms?)" Dr. Li followed up.

My mom answered the question for me.

"She has been sick for about five days now. In the beginning, we thought it was just a regular cold. I have been giving her some medicines for sore throat and fever, but then things started to get worse. Mainly, she has been having a fever and her temperature fluctuates. The peak could be 39°C, and the best number so far has been 38°C. She also feels fatigue, sore throat, headache, and her body is boiling. During the past two days, she started coughing incessantly."

"Ok. I cannot make a conclusion just yet, so we first have to take an X-ray image of your lungs," Dr. Li said with a calm and assertive tone.

"And our goal is to...?" Mom asked for confirmation.

"Based on your description, it is likely that she has the flu, or possibly worse, a lung disease. Her symptoms are also similar to H1N1. An X-ray image would allow me to see what is going on in her lungs, and then I can see what the next steps are," Dr. Li assured Mom.

Mom's face went sullen and my heart sunk when I heard the word "H1N1," also known as "swine flu." My mind instantly jumped to the worst-case scenario of suffering and dying from the infamous disease. Mom was silent, and I could see sweat dripping down her face.

After the doctor got the X-ray image of my lungs, questions spun around in my head. *Would I be okay? What would Dr. Li tell us later? What if I got the swine flu?*

My anxiety and fear were contextualized by the ongoing H1N1 pandemic that ultimately killed almost three hundred thousand people worldwide. My legs were shaking, and my entire body felt icy cold. My veins felt frozen by my overwhelming worry.

***

Dr. Li juxtaposed two enlarged black and white images side by side on a board with spotlights. Mom's and my eyes were glued to the board.

"Here are two images of Mengyao's lungs. One from the front and one from the back. We can see that there are many shaded areas scattered around her lungs." Dr. Li walked us through the images while using his pointer to illustrate the specific spots. "Those shaded areas indicate infections and congestion. These grey areas are more concentrated in her left lung than her right. Any questions so far?"

"So what does this mean exactly?" Mom quickly asked Dr. Li.

"At this point, we still cannot tell if Mengyao has H1N1 or not. We need to do more tests, which could include a blood test and others. This means your daughter will be quarantined at the hospital for a while to receive the tests and treatment," Dr. Li said gravely.

My mom was clenching my right hand, tears in the corner of her eyes. I was frozen on my chair, not knowing how to process this information. For both of us, it was hard to tell which one was worse: uncertainty about my illness or a conclusive answer.

"We have to treat her as if she has the swine flu even if she might not have it. It is better to be safe than sorry. So we need you to sign some paperwork for your daughter before she stays at the hospital for treatment." Dr. Li seemed to read our horrified expressions.

Silence ensued. Mom and I stared at the images as if we could not believe what we just heard. We couldn't speak a word.

My mom finally spoke, her voice shaky. "Thank you, Dr. Li. We will proceed with the next steps. Please do everything you can to make sure my daughter is safe."

Dr. Li patted Mom on her shoulder. "Don't worry. Our whole medical team will take great care of your daughter. We will make sure we try all we can to get her better."

***

My twelve-year-old self was petrified by the idea of quarantine at the hospital.

When we approached the quarantine area, Mom and I started to see scenes that we only saw in movies. There was only one person in each empty room. Each room was hermetically sealed by a door with a small window. While we were passing by, we could glimpse through some of the windows; the inhabitants of the room looked half-dead as they lay on their beds with ventilators covering their faces. From other rooms, we heard ghost-like howling. Thinking I would be living in one of these rooms for an indefinite amount of time made me shiver.

Dr. Li stopped in front of a door and pulled out a keychain to unlock the room in which I would be quarantined. The light was sharp, stinging my eyes with its brightness. The room was spacious with nothing but a big bed in the middle, windows covered to the floor with curtains, and a TV that didn't work.

Maybe this is what quarantine means: living in a vacuum where I could lose the sense of space, time, and maybe eventually, the sense of self. The thought terrified me.

"Most of your time will be spent on this bed because there will be hours of treatments such as antibiotics and oxygen therapy." Dr. Li detailed what I could expect for daily treatments. "These treatments are mainly bottles of liquids that need to be injected into your body. The frequency of the liquid dripping down is usually one second a drop. Every day, you will have a designated nurse to attend to your needs, such as getting meals or going to the bathroom."

While listening to Li's descriptions, I could already visualize my life in the hospital: living like a dead person. Next to my bed, there was a red button, which I assumed was for calling the nurse when I had any urgent needs. Bottles of water were placed on the desk by my bed.

Dr. Li left the room after settling me down. With a surgical mask on, Mom stayed a bit longer until I was almost asleep.

"You just rest, sweetheart. Have a deep and long sleep tonight," Mom whispered while massaging my forehead, relieving some pain from my body. "Don't worry about anything. Dad and I will come to see you as soon as Dr. Li permits."

I wanted to say something back but couldn't. Instead, I started coughing so hard that I spit out yellow and green mucus mixed with blood. Mom quickly brought me water. With the coughing and stinging pain, I could not help but burst into tears. Mom sat by my bed and gave me a heartfelt embrace. I bet Mom was feeling a stab at her heart while she watched me suffer.

"You are strong, Yaoyao! It will get better. I know you can do this."

After the torture of coughing, I ran out of energy, so I fell back on my bed and went to sleep with Mom's goodnight.

***

In my sleep, I felt like I was being swallowed by a dark abyss. Suddenly, a shrill scream from the room next door woke me up. Only a wall separated me and the horrid sound. I opened my eyes and looked around. All I could see was this heavy darkness weighing on me, making it hard to breathe. A thread of pale moonlight streamed into my room through the curtains, casting shadows of the random shapes of the world outside. The shadows crawled on the floor, evoking my darkest fears. It must have been windy outside because the moonlight was shaking and the shadows were moving between the floors and the pale walls. They looked like monsters dancing around, ready to tear me apart.

Was that scream from someone having a nightmare? Are they in pain? Are they dying?

That was the first time I felt so close to death. Home had never felt so out of touch.

The amorphous shadows in my room and my racing thoughts about death made my heart pound so fast. I could hear my breath so clearly it almost sounded like it came from those hideous shadows. Usually, whenever I felt alone and afraid, I curled up with Mom, who would sleep soundly right next to me. However, now there was only me and the deadly silence that could make my worst nightmares come true.

I had no other option to escape this atrocity than closing my eyes and forcing myself to sleep.

When I woke up at 6:00 a.m., the first thing on my agenda was taking the blood test. I did not eat anything the night before and was starving and lethargic. It got worse when I saw my blood run through the tube into the cylinders. I felt lightheaded and almost fainted on the spot.

The sun was already high up in the sky when I returned to my room. A nurse must have also put my breakfast by my bed. Breakfast was simple—a slice of dry bread, a bowl of cold porridge, and a sad-looking apple. My stomach was growling, so I quickly shoveled the food into my mouth. While I was chewing the tasteless food, I could not stop thinking about the steamy wonton soup Mom would have brought me with two soft-boiled eggs.

I missed home. I wanted to be with my parents desperately. I wanted to tell them how scared I had been the night before. I wanted to just be held in their arms and assured that everything would be okay. I wanted to let them know how much I hated this illness that was sucking all the energy out of my once-sturdy body. I did not want to go through this on my own. For the first time in my life, I felt so alone.

After I finished my breakfast, a nurse came in with four huge bottles of liquids.

These must be the treatments that would chain me to my bed for hours during the day. I remembered what the doctor had said about the time-consuming treatments.

"Morning! I am Nurse Ming. You can call me Ming. Starting today, you will be receiving these treatments," Ming said, introducing herself while setting up the equipment.

In her massive mask and long gown, she looked barely human. However, everything on her was pink instead of white. Her pink uniform gave a little life to my pale room.

"Now I am going to inject these liquids into the back of your hands. So clench your hand to a fist and stay still. It might sting and be sore a little bit at the beginning." Ming had a soft and pleasant voice.

"What kind of lung disease do I have?" I struggled to ask Ming with my throat burning.

"It is most likely that you have bacterial pneumonia, which is not contagious. It is a bit better than the viral kind, which is most likely the ongoing H1N1. But we need to do more tests to confirm," Ming said, trying to ease my anxiety.

"How long do you think until I can be discharged from the hospital?"

"It depends on how your body is recovering. People your age usually recover in about a month or two." Ming gave me a better sense of my situation. Then she left the room like a thread of smoke vanished in thin air.

Two months? It seemed like such a long time.

Why did this have to happen to me? Usually when I felt low, I went on a hike or visited the park to refresh my mind. However, neither of those was an option for me. Simply watching a movie was not even an option. I could not even hold a book because both of my hands were being injected into. I even needed assistance to go to the bathroom. All I could do on my own was stare at the off-white walls and ceiling.

Something is cherished even more once it is taken away. The freedom to study, run, and play is one such thing. My immobility made me yearn for the freedom I used to have and took for granted. I missed the days when I could freely breathe without any pain in my throat or congestion in my nose. *The autumn breeze must feel refreshing right now,* I thought. Then the silence reminded me of how much I longed to be with my family. I missed them so much that even those occasional senseless quarrels became endearing.

This first day was indicative of all my upcoming days in quarantine. There was no calendar, no reminder of the outside world, and no trace of life. The earth was spinning, but I did not have a clue. I was just breathing in this vacuum, losing touch with my normal life, even myself. I did not know what was worse: struggling to fight against the new reality or starting to adapt and get used to this period of oblivion as the days passed.

***

One day, when I woke up, my parents were sitting by my bed and gazing at my face.

"Hey, sweetheart, we are here to see you! Dr. Li said you have been doing great and they have managed to at least stabilize your temperature," Mom said with her usual sweet tone mixed with the sound of hope.

"I've brought your favorite kind of yogurt. See? Strawberry flavor. And I got you some fresh fruits to boost your energy. Oranges, apples, and some kiwi fruits." Dad had bags of groceries on his lap and was showing his care package to me.

I thought it was a dream, a very sweet dream I had not had for a long time. But then Dad pinched my cheek and said, "Why do you look so numb? Mom and I are here! Be happy!"

I giggled and smiled back but soon broke out into a cough. Because my lungs were still very weak, whenever I laughed or started talking, a series of deep coughing ensued.

I could see the pain my parents felt while I was coughing out the yellow and green mucus mixed with blood. Without saying anything else, I sat up and hugged them. Their presence brought some light back to my static, repetitive life. Mom handed me an iPad, saying, "I know you are bored to death. Now you can read some books or watch some movies to kill time."

An inexplicable joy spilled all over my heart. Mom's love warmed up this cold and scary place and even made it feel like home.

Dad passed me some peeled oranges and strawberry yogurt. While I was enjoying the fruity flavors, I felt all the long and lonely nights of nightmares vanish into thin air. The smiles on my parents' faces reminded me that I was not alone, and I was loved deeply.

After making sure I was taken care of, Mom and Dad reluctantly left for work. But before they exited my room, they said, "We will be back very soon! We will try to come every other day and alternate. Be good and love you!"

"How long have I been in here?" I struggled to ask this question as my throat hurt.

"It's been a bit over two weeks now. And I think Dr. Li said you need to continue receiving more treatments and tests. The estimated date is hard to tell, but he said around early November," Mom explained.

After my parents left, I was thrown back into the stale vacuum again. However, this time I had the option to do something with my limitless boredom.

I started to reclaim my power over how I spent the hours. Instead of living like a dead person, I put my meandering thoughts into words and typed them into stories on the iPad. Other times, I read books about adventures and traveling to gain inspiration. Reading turned out to be an enriching activity while I was stuck in my quarantine room. The idea of flying away and hopping on an adventure after a trying time inspired me to keep my spirit up. I also proactively cooperated with the medics to help me recover. My new active lifestyle made time insignificant—I no longer cared about what day it was and how much more time I needed to stay at the hospital. I was living in the moment.

***

One morning, Dr. Li woke me.

"Rise and shine! Guess what day it is today?" Li asked with a cheerful and playful tone.

"Umm..." I was still struggling to open my eyes after a deep and sound sleep from the night before.

"Take your time," Li said, still waiting for me to guess.

"Oh no... gotta be kidding..." I rubbed my eyes and excitement bubbled up inside me. "It cannot be *the* day I am free to go home!"

"It can! You did it, Mengyao. You are a very strong girl!" Li cheered and hugged me.

"After we finish some last few steps and feed you well, your parents can pick you up around noon!" Li painted the picture of freedom in front of me.

Tears dripped down my face. I was overjoyed and overwhelmed with emotions. I could not imagine that the illness, loneliness, and endless fears would finally end like this. Flashbacks of staring at the pale walls hopelessly, struggling to sleep many nights, and fighting the excruciating pain flooded back to me.

When my parents walked me out of the place where I had spent two months, I felt a new rush of energy fill my body. I could finally breathe freely again. The absence of home during my time at the hospital made me cherish the time with my family even more. Months of solitude convinced me that I never wanted to feel disconnected from my home again. After battling pneumonia, I felt like a new person.

CHAPTER 5

Dad's Cancer

———

"快回家来。你爸在医院。 (Come home quickly. Your dad is at the hospital,)" Mom said.

I had just stepped out of the last class of the day when I received the abrupt phone call. It was only a few months after I recovered from pneumonia that had chained me to the horrid quarantine room at the hospital for two months. My return to school had not been easy. I had to catch up on months of class materials because there were no recorded lectures and Zoom was not available in 2010. My teachers constantly looked at me with pity and worry. When I was at the hospital, my peers apparently had formed their friend groups, and it was hard for me to join any of them.

Despite these hardships, I thought at least I could put the past two months of struggling behind me. When things seemed to return to normal, my mom's phone call disrupted the rare calmness I had not experienced in a long while.

What happened to my dad? How bad is it? Worried thoughts raced in my head as I ran back home. When I reached the doorsteps, Mom was already in the car waiting for me to hop in. I dropped my backpack in the back seat and sat beside her.

"What's happening?" I tried to catch my breath after racing from school.

Mom put her feet on the pedal and hands on the wheel, eyes glued to the road ahead. She tried to beat the traffic.

"Your dad...He fell on the floor earlier. When I found him, he was curling up with his hands pushing against his lower belly. He was screaming about tormenting pain. I drove him straight to the hospital and then I quickly turned around to pick you up." Mom's voice was shaking.

I clenched my hands as she spoke. Many questions were in my head, but at that moment, I was too shocked and became speechless. Cold sweat dripped down my spine. My whole body braced for the worst to happen.

When we arrived at the hospital, Mom and I sprinted through the aisles and went straight to dad's emergency room.

I almost shrieked when I saw Dad lying in front of me.

Ventilators and many tubes shackled Dad to a pale white bed. His eyes were shut, and his face looked dreary, like a dead leaf. He wore a blue-striped patient gown. His hands and feet looked so delicate and pale. I could see his chest inflate and deflate rhythmically. I looked at the monstrous medical equipment around him and the terror of the situation became real. Never did I imagine Dad could one day be tormented by cancer.

None of the comforts of home surrounded my dad in the cold and white hospital room. My two months spent at the hospital not long ago flashed in front of my eyes.

Mom was standing there with me, hoping that Dad could wake up and see us. The room was deadly silent, and it only added more fear to our hearts. A couple of minutes later, a doctor with a white gown and mask walked in.

"So, doctor, what is it?" Mom swallowed her deepest fear to demand an answer.

"I'm afraid that your husband has liver cancer. He was hurting like that because the tumor had grown and spread out in his body. Not terminal yet, but there are so many complexities that we need to get him treatments without any delay," the doctor said in a solemn voice.

Our worst fear was confirmed.

I stared at the doctor and wanted to scream at him that he was talking bullshit. If only what he said was bullshit. He handed over a couple of MRI images and showed us the tumors inside Dad.

"These are the images we took of Mr. Yuan's liver. As you can see, the dark spots of different sizes are the tumors. I am leading a team of medics to treat Mr. Yuan. We need to do surgery and carve out the tumors while trying not to infect other healthy organs. That's our first step, among others. And we need you to sign some paperwork," the doctor explained to Mom while he pointed to the exact spots of the tumors.

I clenched the MRI image in my hand and felt utterly scared and hopeless. Though the doctor's illustration was thorough and restored a sense of control over the situation, I did not feel assured at all. Even the doctor himself said the other organs could be infected. He also mentioned the complexities of Dad's liver cancer. Certain tumors grew at extremely inconvenient spots, so one small mistake could put Dad in dire condition.

I was unfamiliar with many of the medical terms the doctor used. I stepped closer to the doctor, and the only thing I could say to him was, "Please help my dad. I have only one dad." Tears poured down my face, and I sobbed until I was struggling to breathe.

"I promise we will do everything we can to fight the cancer." The doctor stroked my forehead and tried to calm me down.

The thought of Dad possibly fighting death made me shiver. I could not even start thinking about what my life would be like if he was no longer with me.

The doctor gestured for Mom and I to leave the room so the medic team could prepare for surgery.

During my dad's time at the hospital, my mom and I visited him after school. We did not miss one day, regardless of thunderstorms or snowstorms. Dad ended up battling cancer for a whole year at the hospital. It must have been an extremely lonely and painful experience. I was only stuck in the hospital for two months and it felt like a lifetime to me. I could not imagine enduring the fear and solitude for another ten months, but Dad had no choice.

Each day, we prayed tomorrow would be better, but we all knew it could get worse. The feeling of gambling against fate was unprecedented.

From the day Dad was diagnosed, my life was filled with uncertainty. Fear and insecurity crept into my psyche and haunted me at night. Sometimes I had nightmares of attending my dad's funeral.

I could not concentrate at school because the thought that I might lose my dad at any second consumed me. How could I learn linear algebra when my dad was battling cancer at the hospital?

Every time I visited, I held Dad's hand and shared my achievements at school hoping to cheer him up. Whenever he heard I ranked number one in my exams or I won a debate competition, a subtle smile emerged on his face. Though he was too weak to show much emotion, he tried his best to communicate with me.

Sometimes I sang the songs I learned in my choir. Dad must have loved my songs because one time I saw a tear slide down his cheek. I never saw Dad cry before, except for that one time. I realized even the strongest and most invincible man in my eyes could also have fears.

At times when Dad could speak, he shared all the things he wanted me to remember. He told me to learn to be independent and never let fear get in the way of achieving seemingly impossible dreams. He told me to be strong and keep up with my adventurous spirit even if he was not around. When Dad spoke like that, I always asked him to stop. "Don't say these stupid things. It makes it sound like you are going to leave me. You have no choice but to get better!" I would turn the table and preach to Dad, asking him to remember what I said.

My heart sank when I saw how much my dad suffered from the overwhelming number of treatments. He would growl like an injured tiger and, even worse, cursed at the medics and lashed out in his pain. Dad resented the idea that he was tied to his bed by the bottles of injections. Even the simplest things like eating or going to the bathroom were impossible for him without a nurse's assistance.

One day in the summer of 2010, Mom and I received a call from the hospital.

"Hello? This is Ms. Zhang speaking," Mom said, turning her phone on speaker.

"Mr. Yuan has been recovering well enough to be released from the hospital today. We have ordered prescriptions for him to take at home. His body is still delicate, so be sure to let him rest," the doctor said.

"Wow. Thank you so much for your medical team. I cannot express enough how much it means to our family." Mom burst into tears of joy.

"Of course. That's our job. However, I do need to mention that cancer like this can recur at any time. So we need you to bring your husband here for monthly checkups. And once his condition stabilizes, we can switch to an annual checkup." The doctor tried to set up expectations for Mom so she was not misled.

Once Mom hung up the phone, we blazed our way to the hospital to bring Dad home. I felt the heavy emotional burden that had been torturing me for a year finally vanish. The sleepless nights when I had nightmares about funerals could finally be put to an end. Most of all, my dad could finally be at home with us again.

When the three of us reunited, my dad seemed extremely high-spirited. His face had a healthy blush again. "This calls for a big family feast. My treat!" Dad hollered and took us to his favorite restaurant.

On the way to the restaurant, Dad could not stop sharing with us how grateful and jovial he felt now that he was free from the prison-like hospital room. "身体是革命的本钱！(Health is the foundation for everything!)" He reminded me to always put health as the top priority now that we both had spent an extensive period at the hospital. We did not intend to ever return. He also told me how excited he was to live at home again. Everything felt so right when Dad came back to us because the family was complete.

We had a whole table of food and ate to our hearts' content. While we were enjoying the mouth-watering dishes, I raised a toast to my parents and said, "Cheers to Dad's health and the three of us, an inseparable family!" At that moment, I realized I had come to cherish my home even more than before. Knowing that loss could happen at any moment made me pay more attention to the time I spent with my parents every day. I was grateful to have a complete family.

In the following years, the risk of the cancer coming back was a looming dark cloud that hovered above our heads. Tumors emerged again in Dad's liver two years later, but they were benign and quickly treated. However, Dad's cancer was a constant worry for my family. Not knowing if my dad would need to return to the hospital again for treatment felt like walking on eggshells.

Instead of being concerned about the potential re-emergence of the cancer, Dad focused on improving his wellness with Mom's delicate care. He slept for at least eight hours a day and ate mostly vegetables. My dad went sober and no longer touched one drop of alcohol. Over time, our apprehension faded away as Dad became stronger each day. Because of our immense love for him, Dad had stepped out of the shadow of his liver cancer.

CHAPTER 6

Like Sisters

"唉! 我烦死我妈了, 老是唠叨。(Gosh! I hate how my mom always bitches about the stuff I need to do,)" one of my girl-friends vented to me about her conflicts with her mom.

"I feel like I cannot communicate with my mom any-more. She just does not understand." Another friend told me the tragic truth that she no longer shared her secrets with her mom.

"Are middle-aged ladies always as annoying and nosy as my mom?" Yet another friend of mine complained about the huge generation gap she felt with her mom and how her mom seemed to pry into her life all the time.

However, none of those sentiments existed between my mom and I.

We butt heads sometimes for sure, but even our quar-rels are as heated yet loving as those between sisters. You might wonder how I avoided those problems my friends faced with their moms. One of my childhood anecdotes can shed some light.

After ruthlessly competing through primary school, once I was in middle school, I felt like I could relax a little and breathe for a bit. Granted, middle school was still pretty cutthroat, but girls and boys started their curious exploration of what "girlfriends" or "boyfriends" mean. Crushes were flying around, and you could even smell the bubbly puppy loves floating in the air. My peers were restless. Some passed love notes in class like it was no one else's business, and others sneaked into the secluded garden on campus to enjoy some secret unencumbered moments with their newfound loves.

Love was in the air like the pollen spreading in the spring. Though I had no interest whatsoever in boys, it was hard not to entertain the idea when everywhere I looked, lovebirds were frolicking in twos. Usually, relationships or puppy love in middle school were frowned upon by teachers and parents, even among peers.

"It is distractive! Nothing good will come out of it. Your grades will suffer, and you will see!" our teachers warned us over and over. Their words were powerful because we knew that the dumbest thing to do is to forsake straight As for stupid puppy love.

"We are not fighting this hard to get into the best middle school just so you find your other half!" Mom said, cautioning us about cost-benefit analysis when we were only twelve years old.

"Look who's going to be next to flunk class!" Girls and boys gossiped to see who the fools were sunk in the trap of love.

Ironically, regardless of how harsh these perceptions were toward young lovers, there were always those fierce peers who defied others' opinions and lived the life they wanted. To me, that attitude was liberating.

I was, unfortunately, not exempt from a boy's crush. One casual sunny day in spring 2010, I received a note on my desk after I returned from class.

Hey,

Meet me at the garden after school. I want to talk to you.

The note was short and without a name. I had no clue who wrote it and did not know what to make of it. In fact, it seemed awkward and even a little scary. I grew up in a culture where boys refrained from expressing their feelings to girls openly, and vice versa.

"Boys shouldn't be too expressive and clingy, else they will become too girly," many of my friends' parents would say while they chatted with each other about parenting. With this mindset, it was hard for guys to even lock eyes with girls in a flirtatious way, out of fear they'd be gossiped about. Girls were expected to show affection even less because "you should wait until the boys make the move," as they were often told. Ultimately, no one should make the move or think too much about relationship stuff when they were teenagers. However, the funny aspect of this cultural expectation on relationships is that, after a few years, when their children have graduated from college and start working, parents start to ask, "When are you expecting to get married and have kids?"

We twelve-year-olds had learned very well how to read between the lines while not acting presumptuous. The external pressure from parents and teachers who warned us constantly about the poisonous effects of puppy love made it even harder for middle schoolers to express their affections in a healthy way.

Ding.

My phone got a text notification.

It was from Ming, the troublemaker in our class. He was a tall guy who loved attention more than he loved sports. The way he played basketball was showy, to say the least. Whenever he tried to score, he always made a dramatic leap while his eyes peeked around for admiring gazes from desperate girls. In class, he also took any opportunity to draw eyeballs, sometimes annoying teachers in the process with his disruptive behavior. Making dirty jokes in class or cursing out of the blue were just some of the things he regularly did. My classmates definitely condemned his erratic and sometimes obnoxious personality, but no one could deny or resist his knack for attracting attention.

So there I was, reading a text from troublemaker number one in my class.

Surprised? I like you so I want to talk. Just the two of us.

At first, I thought it was some sort of stupid prank. However, I realized that during class, whenever I turned around, his eyes locked with mine. He could not take his eyes off me. I started to feel butterflies in my stomach.

What do you mean? What for?

I texted back, acting ignorant to mess with him. So after school, I did not go to the garden but returned home immediately.

When I laid down on my couch and took a sip of the cool, freshly squeezed lemonade Mom had prepared for me, my phone started to buzz again.

Where are you?

Why are you not here?

Now I am pissed...

Just when I was staring at my screen and struggling to find a way to reply, my mom passed by and spotted my confused expression.

"Yaoyao, everything okay? What's wrong?" Mom could always tell when something was bothering me. I could hide nothing from her.

"Umm...I don't..." I stammered and did not know how to tell Mom about the troublemaker.

"Who is texting you?" Mom's question was spot on, and nothing could escape her eyes.

I subconsciously tucked my phone under my butt, and said, "Oh, it was nothing."

But I should have known I was a terrible liar in front of Mom. She knows better than thinking everything is fine.

"Honey, I just want to make sure you are okay. Apparently, something is bothering you. You cannot hide it from me." Her words challenged my last line of defense to tell her the truth.

I thought if I told her, she would be mad at me for being distracted by some nonsense from a troublemaking boy. So I still chose not to speak about a thing.

Then Mom's voice started to shake as she said, "I thought we don't hold secrets from each other. Since when do you not want to share your concerns with Mommy?"

Sadness and disappointment were written all over my mom's face. It hurt me to see how my lack of transparency caused her so much distress. Since I was a little kid, Mom was always the person who listened to my worries and guided me through challenging times. Whenever I needed support, I turned to Mom. Nothing was off-limits when my mom and I chatted. When I was juggling dance lessons, piano classes, and literature seminars, Mom was the one cooking meals to fuel me up in between and driving me to different places. She was always there for me.

But in my teenage years, I thought there should be secrets between us. In my head, my mom was a supervisor who would judge my actions and, at times, oppose my decisions. Especially given how much Mom cared about my performance at school, I thought she would be furious to know I did anything that could sabotage my status among the top 10 percent. So to avoid any conflict, I began to learn to hide things from Mom, especially matters that involved boys.

Apparently, I was wrong. Mom still wanted to be my confidant and offer unconditional love and support.

I overcame my fears of Mom's judgments and revealed my conundrum.

"Sorry, Mom. I didn't intend to hide things from you. And I definitely didn't want your feelings hurt. It's about a boy in my class..." I fixated my eyes on the floor and could not look up into Mom's eyes.

"Oh, honey. You think I have never been a twelve-year-old before?" Mom sat down next to me and held me closer so that my head was resting on her shoulder. "What about this boy?" she asked calmly.

"He's that troublemaker in our class. I'm sure you heard about him in parents' meetings. He sent me a note today and asked me to meet him in the garden after class." My face was blushing when I told my mom the truth.

I expected a flurry of accusations and lectures from my mom. I could even hear what I assumed would come next.

How long have you guys been together? How much longer did you plan to hide it from me? You know your grades will slump if you continue, right?

Instead, Mom asked, "How do you feel about this?"

My eyes widened in surprise at my mom's reaction. She'd done the opposite of accusing, and instead, she cared about my feelings.

"Honestly, I feel confused, Mom. I don't know how to respond," I mumbled quietly.

"Do you like him?" Mom asked with a curious smirk.

"I don't know. Maybe I realized I had a little crush on him when he texted and asked me so directly?" My facial expression must have been so bizarre that even my dog, Dots, started barking at me.

Mom picked up Dots from the floor and fondled her belly. "So you like his confidence?" Mom asked.

"Maybe. It's just he is always so sure of himself and so cool. Everyone finds him annoying, but no one can ignore his presence." I hoped Mom wouldn't find my thoughts naive.

"So you like him because he is an attention-seeker?" Mom tried to follow my logic.

When I heard my mom's question, I noticed the absurdity of my thoughts. It was ridiculous how my reason to have a crush on him was feeding into his narcissism. It was crazy how I did not see the problem at the beginning.

Without even voicing her own opinion, Mom helped me unpack the flaws of my own thinking with her questions. I could not find anything to say to fill the silence.

"Well, how are you feeling now?" Mom asked me again.

"I think I will wait for someone who likes me because of me rather than making themselves feel good." I was amazed by the words of wisdom I uttered as a result of my mom's guidance.

Mom smiled proudly and patted my back. "Seems like you figured it out just fine yourself!"

Just like that, I dodged a bullet. Since then, whenever I faced a dilemma in relationships, I have always asked for my mom's opinion. Most of the time, she rarely offered anything but questions that helped me understand myself and the situation better. Even these days, she shamelessly shares with me her funny and stupid past relationships.

Like sisters, Mom and I gossip about boys, go for retail therapy sporadically, or enjoy a weekend getaway in the mountains to spend some mother-and-daughter time.

Due to my dad's constant absence in the house, Mom and I ended up spending a lot of time without him. I started to have fewer and fewer interactions with Dad except occasionally having family dinner together or during the holidays. It occurred to me that my parents started to grow apart as they rarely spent time with each other.

CHAPTER 7

Dad's Temper, Mom's Tears

———

"老爸，这景色太美啦！ (Dad, this view is stunning!)" I was standing above the clouds and looking into the horizon where the sun started to emerge. It was 6:00 a.m., when the sky just started to turn bright, and the temperature was 1°C.

On a clear and sunny day in spring 2005, my family went on a vacation in Yunnan, China. Dad took us on a trip to climb to the zenith of Jade Dragon Snow Mountain, which is about 5,500 meters above sea level. I was only eight years old.

"Told you! The view only gets better if you keep climbing. Now the whole world is under our feet." Dad was so proud he could not stop smiling at me and taking photos with his Canon camera.

Dad's Canon camera did not always bring back sweet memories. When I was eleven, Dad took us to Bali for a couple of weeks in 2008. Dad and I relished finding hidden beaches untouched by any human. We discovered rare shells and caught king crabs or pufferfish. I tried to please Dad by agreeing with his ideas about where to explore next. We hiked in the jungles and tried roasted duck wrapped in bamboo leaves cooked by the locals in a rainforest.

However, out of nowhere, Dad was mad at something Mom said one night. Even during our family vacation, when we were supposed to have fun together, Dad could not control his temper.

"Why do you both always look so grumpy when I want to take photos of you, huh?" Dad yelled at us in our hotel room.

I shivered when Dad directed his anger at me. I did not dare talk back, so I stood silent, timid, and afraid.

"Maybe she's just tired. It's a long day. We've been to many places, so what's so bad if she doesn't want any more photos taken?" Mom tried to defend me with her soft and hesitant voice.

"Shut up!" Dad hollered. His face was imbued with such red fury it looked distorted like a rotten apple.

I wanted to hide somewhere with Mom, but there was nowhere to escape to. We were stuck in the same hotel room with Dad. When I turned my head toward my mom, I clearly saw tears running down her face.

Dad had an explosive temper, the kind that made me want to hide away or made Mom cry. When he was angry, he tended to yell in my face and blasted out his fury on me like a dragon blowing burning flames. He cursed outrageously and crushed the last bit of self-esteem I had. My mom and I had been living with his volcanic temper for years, and we have suffered trauma because of it.

Dad's temper erupted out of nowhere and often occurred when my mom and I disagreed with him. When he discussed what I should do with my life, he vehemently berated me if I refused to take over his art business. When Mom cooked something he didn't like, he threw away his bowl and commanded that she make something else. When he did not like the way I talked, behaved, or even thought, he started roaring like a tiger and shaming me until I couldn't speak a word. Growing up with my dad around felt suppressive, to say the least. Many moments we were supposed to enjoy as a family turned spectacularly dark after he lashed out at us.

I asked Mom frequently why Dad had such a destructive temper, and why she chose to stay with him.

"He had a tragic past. Your dad grew up in a harsh family, and he did not get much love from his parents," Mom said about Dad's difficult childhood.

Dad grew up in a family with three older brothers. He was the youngest, but his parents excluded him the most. Dad grew up at a time when things were drastically different from the environment where I grew up. During the late 1960s to early '70s, most families in China were living a frugal life because the country had just started to develop. Even at a dinner table, there was a limited amount of great food like premium beef for a whole family of six to share. Because Dad was the least favorite among the boys, he always starved and had to go looking for his own food in the middle of the night.

"I try to be as understanding as I can. Every time he cannot control his temper, I try my best to think that it is a consequence of his harsh childhood," Mom always reminded me.

"But how could you live with his outrageous temper for so long? Why didn't you separate from him when I was little?" I asked Mom when I was younger and naive.

"Well, he is your dad. I did not want you to grow up without a dad. Besides, he loves you. It is hard to understand because of his temper, but he does," Mom explained whenever I questioned her about her choice.

Mom's words always sunk me into deep thoughts about my conflicting feelings for Dad and his relationship with Mom. The love between my parents was definitely confusing. I believe Mom could only endure Dad's monstrous temper for my sake and to have a complete family. As for Dad's love for my mom, I had very little sign of it except for the fancy gifts he showered Mom with.

I learned to convince myself of Dad's elusive love for me despite his explosive temper. I tried not to take Dad's angry words to heart. However, no matter how much I wanted to believe the most beautiful form of love Dad had for this family, my belief was shadowed by his uncontrolled temper and the many excruciating times when he made Mom cry.

It was hard for me to grapple with Dad's thoughts and emotions because sometimes he seemed approachable—as if his temper never existed. Interacting with him was like cautiously walking on eggshells—I never knew when what my mom or I said could trigger his anger again.

The memories of his explosive temper created pain in my brain, so I would rather continue recalling the good times. My thoughts returned to the peak of Jade Dragon Snow Mountain.

The view was indeed magical. Clouds surrounded us and formed many shapes. We spotted formations that looked like a phoenix, a boat, and a jet plane. Among the layers of clouds, we could still see other mountaintops emerge from the mystic aura. They were all covered in milky white snow as if those mountaintops were vanilla ice cream cones. The clouds, the snow, and the sweeping view of the mountaintops came together and displayed a spectacular show in front of us. There was a sublime and powerful ambience all around us.

Mom, Dad, and I could not help but stand there, completely speechless, and try to take everything in. The sun was slowly rising on the horizon and painted the Eastern corner of the sky with a bright gold color and shimmering pink and orange. We had woken up before the roosters and climbed up the mountain when the sky was still dark so we could catch the sunrise the moment we made it to the top.

Though I was carried away by the stunning view in front of me, my mind was still dwelling on the challenging journey from the bottom of the mountain to the peak. Darkness impeded us from seeing the path clearly, and it was very easy to slip and fall because ice and snow spread out on the mountain range. The wind got stronger as we pushed against it and headed upward. Our ears popped a few times, and we started to feel lightheaded because of the elevation.

Regardless of the strenuous climb, Dad was behind me every step of the way. He sometimes pushed me up when I was about to fall back. When I felt tired and discouraged by the howling wind, lightheadedness, and darkness, Dad sat down with me on a rock and wrapped his jacket around me to keep me warm. When I breathed so heavily I could not voice my discomfort, my dad went ahead of me and dragged me up through the rocks so I never needed to look back down again. He reminded me, "You can do it! You are so brave and have made it this far!"

Dad's boost powered me through over 5,500 meters up into the sky, despite my fear of heights and disbelief in my own potential. When I was on top of the mountain, I thought Dad's love for me was just like the rising sun above the clouds. It warmed up the cold air with gold sunrays and beamed through my heart to give me energy.

When asked how I feel about Dad's love, I still say it feels like I am on a summit, overlooking the earth beneath and the sun rising on the horizon.

That was only one memory among the many good times when Dad and I felt close to each other. Perhaps the beauty of the good times is that they feel like an eternity. Over time, I noticed the change in Dad's presence in my life.

Dad's love started to feel elusive. One reason was that his explosive temper made it challenging to approach him; another reason was that I spent much more time with Mom because he was not always home. His gradual absence from my daily life further estranged our connection. His involvement in my life started to fade toward the end of my time at middle school.

"Is Dad going to come home today?" I asked Mom one day after I got home from school.

"Um... honey, I don't know. He needs to be at the villa for a few days. It's closer to his art gallery, you know?" Mom lamented in an aloof tone while preparing dinner in the kitchen.

"To do what?" I unpacked my backpack in the living room and found Mom's description extremely weird.

"He said he's busy these days. Many client dinners to attend and lots of meetings with his staff at the art gallery to prepare for the upcoming exhibits." Mom raised her voice across the room. She sounded like she wished the reality was different, but she had no control over it.

"I see. I mean he rarely comes home now. Like once or twice a week at most? Over the weekend if we are not going to the villa, then we do not see him at all." The more I complained about Dad's absence, the more pissed off I was. Most of the time, he did not even tell Mom or I what exactly he was doing.

Ring. Ring.

Our house phone buzzed. I ran over and picked it up.

"Hello?" I said, waiting for the other side to speak.

"Hey! How's school today?" It was Dad. He tried to sound like he cared even though he was not there with Mom and I.

"It's fine. Busy as usual. How about you?" I tried to probe why Dad rarely came home.

"The usual business stuff. Many dinners to attend and things to set up for the art gallery," he replied with a cursory response so brief it made me feel nosy to ask further.

"Well, when are you going to come home again?" I felt there was no need to beat around the bush, so I asked the question that really mattered.

"Honey, I will try. Maybe this weekend you and Mom can come to the villa? It will be great for you to get away from all the schoolwork and relax." Dad's talent in language was indisputable. He had a way of covering up his absence from this family with a nice diversion I could hardly track.

"Errrr... okay." There was nothing else left for me to say.

"Be good. Miss you." Dad's words somehow touched the softest part in my heart, as if he was speaking for me.

"Miss you too. Maybe come home for dinner sometimes." I felt like there was no need to try to convince him of anything else. Sometimes he did come home for dinner, but rather sporadically. Even if he did have dinner with us, he had to leave right after. He always seemed so busy, and most of the time, I had no idea how his life suddenly got so hectic.

Dad's love was fleeting and felt even more out of touch these days now that I am on the other side of the world. We only speak with each other on video chats once or twice a month. On top of that, my relationship with Dad was shaken by his betrayal of Mom. Ever since, there's been an unspeakable wound in my trust for him, and neither of us tries to elaborate on it. It would be so painful to be vulnerable and admit to each other how our bond has changed by the divorce.

Though I know how evasive his love can be, I still would like to believe it has been here with me all along. I miss the dad who makes me feel like I am at the top of a mountain, with the whole world under my feet.

CHAPTER 8

A Lone Wolf in Israel

___

What does being a young adult mean anyway? I wondered while eating my eighteenth birthday ice cream cake on April 14, 2015.

As I was pondering the question about adulthood, an urge to do something daring emerged in my mind.

I pulled out a world map on my laptop and marked the countries I had visited. My cursor was meandering around and landed in the Middle East region. I realized I had never been to Israel. Some of my Jewish friends told me bits and pieces about *Chutzpah* in Israeli culture and said they saw some *Chutzpah* in me. I had no clue what they were talking about, so I thought, *why not spend a summer in Israel?*

Dad used to tell me the best way to learn about a culture is to learn its language. I started searching online for summer language programs offered at universities in Israel.

The Hebrew Ulpan program for beginners at Tel Aviv University (TAU) popped up at the top of my search. As a city girl, I wondered if I could see smart architectures and have the comfort of home at my fingertips in Tel Aviv. From a few Google images, I gathered that skyscrapers carve out the silhouette of the skyline in Tel Aviv and the city has ample options for entertainment. I decided to apply for a visa, book my flight, and go to Israel.

My family vacations had not been happening for a while, and it seemed that Dad became more and more absent from the family with his late-night dinners or other "business reasons." Throughout my three years in high school, Dad did not take Mom and I on vacation anywhere outside of the country. Every previous trip we took together, my dad's hot temper turned what would have been a relaxing vacation into a stressful endeavor. My adventure to Israel would be my first solo trip internationally, without constantly worrying about pleasing my dad.

My dad inspired me to be a fearless solo traveler, and I ended up inheriting his independent spirit to get away from him. I felt relieved and excited to break away from my home for a while.

My parents did not support my idea at the beginning because they thought I was ignorant about how dangerous it could be to travel on my own, especially in Israel. However, I had already gotten my travel visa, booked my flight, and arranged my stay at Tel Aviv University without telling them. I was determined to go, and there was no way back.

I packed light and fitted three months of essentials into a mini luggage bag and hopped on an El Al plane.

My heart was pounding fast as the plane took off. I had no idea how the three months in Israel would unfold. When the plane was flying above the clouds, I knew that worrying about the future would not help me enjoy my adventure. So I did what Dad used to remind me to do, sit back and relax.

When I landed at Ben Gurion airport, it was already past midnight on June 16. The moment we touched the ground, the whole plane of passengers with kippahs on their heads broke into thunderous and unified applause. I was confused about what was happening. The lady sitting next to me said it's a thing people do when they return to Israel.

I rubbed my eyes and tried to wake myself up from the nap I'd taken during the flight. The moment I stepped off the plane and into the airport to pick up my luggage, I realized people were aggressively wrestling their way past me. The atmosphere was full of tension, and it made me feel nervous and alert.

It took about an hour to find my luggage. When I checked the time, it was already 2:00 a.m. I tried to fight my sleepiness and continued to find my way to TAU. When I walked out of the airport, a gust of cool summer breeze woke up my senses. I anxiously looked for signs that said "taxi." After asking a stranger, it turned out I had to take a train to get to where I needed to go.

I dragged myself toward the train platform and impatiently waited for the next train to come. No one waited on the platform but me. It was deep into the night, and I was on guard the whole time. A black cat appeared in front of me, and the surroundings looked no different from a thriller or a horror movie—dark, quiet, and ominous.

About half an hour later, a train arrived. It seemed like my last thread of hope to rescue me from the horror-movie scene. At that point, not only was my body screaming to rest, but my brain was exhausted from staying alert at such an ungodly hour. I could not see anyone else on the entire train.

My eyelids become heavier as I struggled to stay awake. The repetitive noise from the railroad in the background quickly put me to sleep. When I woke up again, I had no idea where I was. Apparently, it was the last stop, so I had to get off. I stumbled out of the train and made sure the luggage was still with me.

I lost myself again in a strange place. It was already almost 4:00 a.m., so no one was around. I did not know where to go, so I followed along the main street and found an apartment building. Without a second thought, I entered its lobby and decided to first rest and then figure out how to get to TAU later. I collapsed on a chair and held my luggage as a support so I could rest my arms on it. I closed my eyes again and quickly fell asleep.

When I woke up again, it was already 7:00 a.m. About ten minutes later, a bus showed up in front of the apartment building. When I saw it, I quickly gathered my stuff and ran outside. When I hopped onto the bus, I realized no one else spoke English anymore, so I had to say "ביבא לת תטיסרבינוא (Tel Aviv University)" to the driver. That was pretty much everything I knew in Hebrew.

Sweat dripped from my forehead to my chin. My heart raced faster as I anxiously hoped the driver understood me. The air was humid, and it made me feel like I was stuck in a sauna. I even pointed at my backpack to indicate to the driver that I was a student.

He repeated again for me to confirm, and he nodded with a welcoming grin. It was crazy that he understood me! After fifteen minutes or so, he dropped me off in front of the dorm.

When I saw a big sign that said, "Einstein," I knew I was at TAU's Einstein dorm. I started laughing hysterically to let out the stress and exhaustion I had experienced throughout the hectic transit. I quickly contacted the dorm director and moved into my room.

I had no idea that the hectic experience of getting to TAU was just the beginning of a series of wild travels as a young eighteen-year-old girl in Israel.

Over the first two weeks in the Hebrew Ulpan program, I managed to make some friends among my classmates. I quickly connected with Julia and Autumn because we often strived to be the first to answer questions. I thought that לפאלפ (Falafel) and המראווש (Shawarma) tasted better when shared with friends, and exploring synagogues and historic landmarks became more and more enjoyable with the three of us together.

Julia and Autumn invited me for a few sleepovers at their apartment close to the city square in Tel Aviv. We shared many fun moments together. During the weekdays, we cooked dinners together, and over the weekends, we biked around Tel Aviv or along the gold coastline of וודרוג ףוח (Gordon Beach). Some nights, if we felt daring, we stormed into a nightclub and danced to loud music until we were too tired to jump around in heels.

About halfway through my time in Israel, my new friends and eventful days made me realize that I'd started rooting myself and building a new life in this foreign place.

A decent amount of people in the program were also recent high school graduates going to college in the fall. Many of them, as I learned, were on Birthright, all-expenses-covered trips to Israel.[4] Because of our age group and shared excitement for the college years ahead, we ended up taking a mud bath at the Dead Sea and spending a whole week in Jerusalem.

My initial anxiety about traveling alone in Israel started to fade away as I went on more and more adventures. Three months in a new place no longer seemed impossibly long to me. When thrown into a place where I had no relatives or any connections, I was pushed to proactively reach out to people and mingle. I believed my instinct to survive made me impressively eager to socialize with strangers.

When not surrounded by my new friends, I loved losing myself with the locals. One day, I hopped on a bus without a destination in mind and an old lady sat across me. At first, I felt nervous about speaking with anyone around me, but I thought: *I did not learn Hebrew for two months just so I could not speak a word. The bus ride will take a while, so why not chat with a local?*

The old lady stared out the window. She wore a colorful floral silk scarf, a cotton sundress, and a pair of dark brown sandals. Her skin was tanned and reflected the color that almost matched her sandals. Her hair was short, curly, and mostly grey. She seemed to be immersed in her own world, indifferent to the chatter around her.

I had to try several times to lock eyes with her.

---

4   Leila Ettachfini, "What Is Birthright and Why Is It So Controversial?" *Vice*, August 15, 2019.

"יתרבג םיבוט םיירהצה רחא!)" (Good afternoon, ma'am!)" I spoke every word carefully, with a beam of friendliness.

"רמולש המ! םולש?)" (Hello! How are you?)" The lady responded with surprise. Her eyes sparkled like the shimmers dancing among the waves in the Mediterranean Ocean.

"התאו.רדסב ינא?)" (I'm good. And you?)" I tried to remember the lines I learned in the lecture earlier this morning. By this point, I just hoped she wouldn't suddenly say something way beyond my comprehension.

"רמ֫ש֫ה תַמ. רע אל ימולש?)"(Not bad. What's your name?)" She leaned forward so she could hear me better.

"םירמ. תאו?)" (Mary. What's yours?)"

So far so good. I thought.

"לארשיל ךתוא איבמ המ. רעה אל ךלש תירבעה. הנשוש?)" (Shoshana. Your Hebrew is not bad. What brings you to Israel?)" The lady started to speed up.

I did not think I followed her completely. For a second, I forgot what "איבמ" meant. My brain started to visualize the pages of notes I took in class. I knew it had to be a verb because I knew the rest of her sentence. "Errr... ahh..." I stuttered and scratched my head.

Come on, Mary. You know this. It shouldn't be this hard. So much for "Your Hebrew is not bad," I thought.

The Israeli grandma chuckled and repeated her question slowly.

"ץיקה ביבא לת תטיסרבינואב ןפלוא תינכתב תירבע דמול ינא !הא." (Ah! I'm studying Hebrew in the Ulpan program at Tel Aviv University this summer.)" A light bulb went on in my head. I was so relieved that the notes I took did not go to waste. Phew!

"וישכע דלוה התא ואל. םימישרמ?" (Impressive. Where are you going now?)" Shoshana followed up.

"גשומ יל ןיא." (I have no idea.)" I shrugged my shoulders.

Shoshana seemed amused by my spontaneity, or more like "lack of a plan." We chatted for a few more minutes, and she said, "לארשיב ינהית!" (Have fun in Israel!)" as I stood up from my seat.

I hopped off at a stop and had no idea where I was. It turned out I was close to ופי (Old Jaffa), the old city that existed before Tel Aviv was born.

When I found myself all alone again, my instinct to connect with strangers activated again. I saw a guy who seemed to be waiting for someone, so I asked if he knew the best way to explore Old Jaffa.

He gave me a sly grin and said, "You are lucky. I'm a guide myself. Right now, I am with a group of people, but come back tomorrow and I will show you everything there is to see here."

I can't be this lucky! I told myself. However, a deep voice from the heart of Old Jaffa whispered to me, "Yes, you can!"

The next day, I explored the mysterious city built with dark orange-color bricks with the local guide whose name was ןתנ, (Natan). Old Jaffa exuded a quaint and captivating aura. With antique cafes or craft shops tucked in small valleys and walls, it was a sweet combination of the old world and the new. Occasionally, I stumbled onto couples taking wedding photos.

As I paced myself through the pebble path between the walls, I lost myself among the various architectures. The narrow and intricate paths entwined in and out of different corners of the fortress-looking establishment. It was like a maze, and it made me feel like I was weaving in and out of history. My feet were firmly rooted on the ground, and I let the sacred energy infuse my body. Throughout my walking tour, Natan and I let my instinct lead the way as if Old Jaffa had a built-in magnet from the ancient time that pulled me in certain directions. I simply followed where my heart took me.

I was in awe of the stunning views of the old town that overlooked the Mediterranean Sea, but my joy came mostly from savoring my time in a foreign land all by myself. I could no longer travel with my family without confronting my dad's explosive temper, but at least now I could travel solo without any conflicts and tensions. However, I still missed the beautiful family vacations when my parents and I cherished our time together as one happy unit. When Dad traveled with us without a temper, he was particularly endearing and loving—and I missed that side of him.

When I was at the highest point of Old Jaffa and overlooked the waves rushing to the shore from the middle of the ocean, the question I had at my eighteenth birthday came back to me. Eighteen meant the start of independence, so my parents say, but independent from what?

The ocean breeze kissed my cheeks, and my hair flowed freely. The sun started to set by the horizon and painted the sky a mixture of vanilla cream color, flamingo pink, and flame red.

My Hebrew teacher in the Ulpan program explained the meaning of "Chutzpah" during the lecture yesterday. It means bold, audacious, and fearless, which became my way of living in Israel. Though I adored the time I spent with my new friends, I felt in sync with myself when I was a lone wolf wandering aimlessly to an unknown destination. Where I was going was not important, but continuously exploring solo on the road opened me up to new encounters and fresh perspectives on my old questions.

As I was mesmerized by the spectacular view in front of me, the answers to the question popped up in my mind. Maybe what people told me about independence meant the ability to create a home wherever I go. Maybe it meant independence from the one home I had my entire life.

I spread my arms open and took a deep breath, with my eyes closed. I felt like I was a bird flying into the sunset, as high in the sky as I wanted and as free as I could be.

I could not think of a better eighteenth birthday gift for myself than traveling solo in Israel for three months.

CHAPTER 9

The Other Side
of the Pacific

The summer I spent in Israel gave me a taste of how independent I could be living away from home. I managed to stay safe
while trying to find my way back from Haifa to Tel Aviv on a
midnight train. I also saved myself from danger and injuries
when a violent protest erupted in the city square. By the end
of the three months, I made it back to my family in one piece.

However, I didn't realize at the time that my solo travels
in Israel were only the beginning of years living abroad alone.
Less than two weeks after I landed home safely, it was time
to pack my luggage again for college over seven thousand
miles away in Atlanta. A summer spent in Israel was not
long enough for me to feel homesick. Every day, I was busy
studying Hebrew, making new friends, and sipping ראטסדלוג,
Goldstar beer on the beach with Julia and Autumn. When
the summertime in Tel Aviv started to feel long, I turned to

my calendar and realized I had only a few more days to go before I returned home.

My transition to college across the other side of the world would be different. Spending four years in a completely foreign country meant I needed to build my life there, without any friends or family to begin with. I could only imagine the loneliness I would feel and the intense longing to return to my family. Never had I fathomed being away from home for years on my own.

It was August 16, my dad's birthday, and also five days before my flight to Atlanta. Mom reserved a table at Dad's favorite restaurant. She ordered a customized birthday cake for Dad a few days prior. We knew it would likely be the last time I could celebrate my dad's birthday with them for the next four years. Summers during busy college years would be filled with internships and study abroad programs.

With that thought in mind, the three of us tried to enjoy the moments together when we could. I don't recall much about the soup dumplings scattered all over the big, round dinner table, but I remember the conversations I had with my parents that lasted for hours.

"瑶瑶，你妈和我不在你身边儿，这次你得学会独立啦。(Yaoyao, it is time that you learn to live on your own and take care of yourself without your mom and me around,)" Dad started his speech while munching on his spring rolls.

"Your dad is right. We will always be worried about you. So you need to learn to take care, choose your friends, and stay healthy," Mom also chimed in while eating a slice of Peking duck mid-bite.

I could see in my parents' eyes their concerns about sending me across the Pacific for four years of college. I could also sense their sadness that I was about to be so far away from them so soon.

Where did the time go? Suddenly, I became a young adult with the whole world before me.

I bet they were thinking about the same thing.

We were dining in a private room, so our heartfelt conversation made the ambiance especially intimate and emotional.

"You are a grown-up now. There will be times when you will need to make decisions for yourself and you won't have your mom and I immediately offering our opinions. So you have to start learning to analyze certain tough situations on your own," Dad continued with a deep yet gentle voice. While he was talking to me, his eyes stayed locked on mine the whole time. Every word from his mouth demanded my full attention. I could also see Mom was about to cry as the emotional dinner conversation went on. I could see through her eyes the high hope and pride my mom felt for me.

"I think the past eighteen years, we have developed your solid character and I have confidence that you can take it from here. I trust that you will make the best out of your college years ahead," Dad said.

I could not hold back my feelings anymore. "Mom, Dad, I want to thank you for raising me and providing so many amazing opportunities for me to thrive. I am truly grateful."

Mom, and, to my surprise, even my dad, burst into tears of joy. I rarely saw Dad cry, but at that moment, he could not hold in his emotions. I could see the immense love my parents had for me. On one hand, they longed to be with me; on the other, they wanted me to start my own journey.

We recounted the anecdotes and highlights starting from when I was a baby up through high school. My parents' eyes lit up when they relived the stories of my growth over the past eighteen years. They started from the grand piano Dad bought me for my third birthday; then they mentioned how much they were impressed by my courage to learn swimming with Dad in the ocean at age four. They went on recollecting our family vacations in Indonesia. My parents commended me for my curiosity and decision to pursue college away from home. The vivid details from my parents' memories expressed their subtle care every step of the way as I grew up.

The history of my family and the essence of my identity fleshed out in my parents' recollections. I hoped those anecdotes would guide me like a compass as I stepped into the new chapter of my life filled with excitement, unknowns, and many more memories waiting for me to create.

Five days later, I headed to the airport with my luggage and the stories my parents remembered by heart. My parents and I had breakfast at the airport before I passed through the security checkpoint. This time, they both became surprisingly taciturn. I knew they wanted to tell me so much more, but I figured they wanted to enjoy the last few minutes of togetherness before I flew away. When it was about time for me to leave, I slowly trudged toward security with Mom and Dad. At the point where they could go no further, I turned around and held my parents in my arms. Tears dripped down my face.

"Mom, Dad, don't you worry. I will take care of myself and remember all the things you told me," I reassured them.

Reluctantly, I walked away from them through security. I looked back, and they were still standing there waving at me with their brightest smiles. They nodded at me and gestured for me to keep moving forward. When I passed security and looked back again, lines of crowds blocked my view, and I could not see if my parents still stood there.

That's when I realized it was time to not look back but only look forward.

***

The flight from Beijing to Atlanta was long, with a layover in Detroit for about sixteen hours. Passing through the customs maze was not fun either as I pushed through the serpentine crowds.

People slowly moved forward to get stamps on their documents from the officers. Many travelers looked worn out and especially anxious when some staff hustled them to step forward. Occasionally, the airport staff spoke impatiently and even rudely to the passengers who walked sluggishly but were too tired to talk back.

The feeling of foreignness and otherness could not be more apparent when I noticed the stark contrast between the "foreign visitors" lane and the "US citizens and green card holders" lane. The former, which I was stuck in, was long and packed; whereas the latter, which I was staring at, was quick and convenient—no one was stuck like the people around me were. Maybe it indicated a bigger metaphor that foreshadowed living in the US—non-citizens can expect to encounter inconvenience, rude treatment, and other challenging conditions, but citizens are entitled to comfort, respect, and prestige.

It was definitely not home anymore.

When I looked up, very few people looked like me; the ones who looked remotely like me were not my friends or family. The officer greeted me with a poker face, which seemed to be a common facial expression among the airport staff. At least he did not give me a hard time. I finally got a stamp on my passport, walked hastily away from the area, and picked up my three heavy luggage bags. After hours of navigating that labyrinth, replete with anxious people and unwelcome inquisition, I was eventually freed. I did not want to spend one more second in that hectic place.

Exhausted, utterly sleep-deprived, and thirsty, I made it to my room at Emory.

I got to my room around 10:00 p.m. As I looked around, I saw everything new and unfamiliar—a city that seemed smaller than my hometown, a campus that I had only seen on their website, and a room so empty and quiet. Everything looked like a blank canvas waiting for me to splatter colors on it. In fact, my whole college life was ahead of me and waiting for me to create it. I had no idea what to expect, but I knew I would find out with my intense enthusiasm to build my experience from scratch.

Though the room needed a makeover, my body was about to collapse. I resolved to save tomorrow's problem for tomorrow.

The first semester started with a flurry of events—attending orientation, bonding with my roommate, signing up for classes, rushing for sororities, and keeping up with my nineteen-credit coursework. I spontaneously signed up for the student newspaper and Emory Polo club. To be honest, I was clueless about how my social life would turn out. Rushing for sororities was purely out of curiosity. Little did I know it was a hectic, draining, and discriminatory process, the opposite of what I needed to find a sense of belonging, which required an accommodating environment.

Building a sense of belonging was trying. For the first time, I learned about the isolating experience as a minority, a term I had never identified myself with before. Domestic students were the majority, and very few showed an interest in the challenges that international students had to go through—homesickness, cultural shock, and loneliness.

I knew I was far away from home when I was very self-conscious about how different I was from everyone else around me. My first impression about domestic students was that they were very loud, a mannerism I was not accustomed to. I realized I had to be extra proactive to get heard, to make friends, and to secure opportunities to speak in class. If I was the minority, I knew I had to work harder than my peers to get accepted by the clubs I signed up for, to achieve high academic performance, and to find the communities where I could feel I belonged.

My realization inspired much of my curiosity and drive to learn, and the Chutzpah I inherited during my time in Israel resurfaced.

I pushed myself to embrace each day with abundant enthusiasm and energy, which later led me to become the founder of a coffee club on campus. It was a social enterprise initiative that delivered fair-trade coffee to students' dorms. The small business was considered ethical because we gained supply from farmers who produced the coffee beans and made sure they directly profited from the sales without any middlemen reaping off a fraction. Unexpectedly, I got a bid from my sorority and became one of the founding members responsible for designing philanthropy events.

Among all of these commitments, making new friends was also my priority. My roommate, Alaina, and I became very close. We connected through our shared passion for the arts—Alaina played violin, and I relished singing thanks to my voice training in the choir. Though our class schedules did not overlap, we still made time every week to at least have three meals together with some other hall mates. Thanks to my coffee business, many peers in my dorm started to become friends with me. Over the weekends, a group of five to eight chipper college freshmen would brunch at a chic café downtown or attend a music festival at a park.

Gradually, without me realizing it, my close-knit group of friends became the family I had away from home. We ate together, crammed late-night papers together, embarked on adventures in the city together, and took care of each other.

One Thursday night, after I returned to my room after my last evening lecture, I flopped onto my bed. My head hurt, my muscles ached, and my body boiled. Deeply lethargic, I felt my eyelids get heavy. When I was sick and alone, I missed my family dearly. Usually, my parents would give me medicine and help me recover. Mom would hand me a bowl of steamy noodles and Dad would give me a bottle of cool strawberry yogurt, which is my favorite. Before bed, Mom made sure I took the medicine and went to sleep early.

Memories of my parents' visits to the hospital when I was battling pneumonia in the quarantine room flashed before my eyes. A few piercingly painful coughs brought me back to my cold and lonely room. I looked around but only saw furniture—no one was there to look after me when I needed them most.

Tears dripped down my chin and dropped on my pillow. I quietly laid on my bed, without even the slightest strength to go outside and get medicine.

My roommate was not in the room, so I texted Asma, another great friend I hung out with regularly.

Oh no! I'm in the lab, but I will be right there! Asma texted me back.

No longer than ten minutes later, Asma showed up in my room. She gasped when she saw me, "Oh, Mary! You look like you are burning up. You might have a fever. Let me first get you some hot tea, and then I will run to CVS to get you some Tylenol."

She sat on the edge of my bed and placed her left hand on my forehead and then on the side of my neck. Asma frowned and looked worried. "You are boiling, Mary! Yes, you definitely have a fever. Just try to take a nap and I will be right back! And...why is your pillow wet?" Asma's hand landed next to my ear.

"I feel horrible. And I miss home..." I whispered.

"Aww, Mary. I can only imagine how you feel right now—feeling sick and far away from home. But, hey, I promise that you will feel better once I return with some tea and medicine." Asma said, trying to cheer me up as she stood up.

Her thoughtfulness and kindness warmed my heart and reminded me of the feeling of home and family who were always there when I needed them.

When I woke up from my nap, Asma was sitting in front of me with a cup of hot honey lemon tea and a CVS bag.

"Here, take two pills with a sip of tea." She helped me sit up on my bed.

Asma's delicate care of me reminded me of my mom. After a sip of the lemon tea, I said, "I really appreciate it, Asma. I cannot thank you enough for doing this." I could feel love alleviate the pain of my fever.

"Don't mention it, Mary! This is what friends are for. I can't bear to see you half-dead on your bed! Haha." Asma said, brightening up my day. Then she reached out and gave me an assuring hug.

I was beyond grateful that I had such an amazing friend like Asma who treated me like family and made me feel at home away from home. My life at Emory felt more and more natural to me, and I was lucky to have many friends like her.

***

Alaina took me back to her home in Los Angeles. I could not have imagined that I would build a sense of home so quickly only two months into my first semester. While I was in her hometown, Alaina and I had burgers and fries at In-N-Out, got manicures, shopped at the Grove, dipped our toes in the chilly ocean water at Santa Monica, and visited the Getty Museum. She showed me around the best of Los Angeles, and we had a crazy fun time soaking ourselves in the West Coast sunshine and ocean breeze.

For the first Thanksgiving in college, I would not have anywhere else to celebrate. I felt grateful when Alaina brought me to her family's Thanksgiving dinner. She had a large family. The dinner table accommodated about seventeen people, with her aunts and uncles and her cousins. It was the first time I felt the warmth of home after I left Beijing. Everyone was dressed up and merry. The chats at the dinner table could get very loud and boisterous, and they reminded me of the dinner table chats I used to have with my family during the Spring Festival.

An apple-stuffed turkey was lying in the middle of the long redwood table. My favorite dish was the green bean casserole and the mashed potatoes with sausage gravy. In a completely different home, I felt welcomed and appreciated the hospitality expressed by Alaina's family.

As much as Alaina tried to make it feel like home for me, I thought about my family a few nights and became homesick. Alaina's large and dynamic family reminded me of my own, and I realized they were so far away. Even when I wanted to video call my parents sometimes, because of the time difference, they were already asleep.

My freshman year flew by as I juggled numerous activities and courses. Never could I have imagined that I would fall in love with polo, become a beat reporter for the newspaper, and establish a popular coffee business. However, when the world quieted down at night, and my dim bed light was on, my yearning for home started to torture me. Though I could not physically be with my family, the best I could do was text my parents, ask how they were doing, and tell them I missed them dearly. When I woke up the next morning, I would throw my sadness aside and keep my feelings to myself.

By spring 2016, my homesickness had faded away. I realized my new home transformed into the new life I built at Emory. The realization I had at the airport came back to me: *don't look back, keep looking forward.*

PART 3

LOOKING FOR HOME GLOBALLY

"I am going on a pilgrimage around
the world to search for home and find
my answers."

CHAPTER 10

My House No Longer Feels Like Home

———

Atlanta welcomed its first snow of the year around December 2016. Christmas was still a few weeks away, but the festive campus already hinted at the upcoming joyful time celebrating family and love. Undergraduates packed their luggage and promised each other to "hop on FaceTime soon" or "keep up with my Insta." After hugging friends and reluctantly walking separate ways, some loaded their cars and hit the road, and others hopped on a Lyft to the Hartsfield-Jackson Airport. My college peers left the hard-earned and eventful semester behind and headed to one place—home.

I, on the other hand, did not quite share their joy and excitement. I was enjoying the ivory kingdom for a fleeting moment until it dawned on me that winter break meant returning to a broken home, the last place I wanted to be.

The last phone call I had with Mom—when she broke the news of my parents' divorce a couple of months ago—was the only time I had talked to anyone from home. For over two months, I had managed to at least make it through the semester, however lost and emotionally drained I was. Now I had to confront my worst fear—seeing how shattered my family was with my own eyes.

What was supposed to be a long-anticipated and overdue reunion filled with joy became a suffocating burden and a nightmare. I used to hate that it takes about eighteen hours to fly back to Beijing from Atlanta, but then I hated that it didn't take longer. It was tragic, but what options did I have?

All the complex and piercing emotions flooded back— anger, confusion, fear, sadness, and immense pain. Many questions raced through my head as I stared out of the plane's window.

How would I react when I first saw my dad again? What would I say to him with all my rage and questions? Would both my mom and dad still be there together to pick me up at the airport? Where could I hide if I could not take the pain of being there in person anymore?

I simply did not know the answers.

I felt like a doomed lamb trapped by wolves, waiting for the worst attacks from the painful reality unfolding in front of me. Before I tried to figure out how to react to my parents, the plane landed.

After I pushed through security, customs, crowds, and reached the arrival level, I saw two familiar figures standing by the end of the queue waiting. As I approached them, my heart raced, not from excitement like before, but from fear.

There they were, my mom and my dad. When I could see them closer, I was stunned by how many more wrinkles appeared on their faces—exhaustion and fatigue written all over them. More grey hair also showed around their foreheads. They looked like they had just fought an excruciating battle, not by each other's side but rather against each other. Like Terracotta soldiers, they just stood there, cold and stern, without words or emotions.

"这来啦! 快抱抱妈妈。(There you are! Come here and give me a big hug.)" Mom was the first to move toward me with her usual loving smile and arms wide open. Although this time, her smile was overcast by a layer of sadness.

Our embrace was interrupted when Dad approached me. He briefly made eye contact with me and picked up my luggage, taking big strides toward the exit to the car. I did not have enough time to even take a good look at him. All I could see was his back and silhouette. Despite all the things he had done to cause Mom and I tremendous pain, at that moment, all I wanted was to look at him. He was so out of reach.

He walked way ahead of my mom and I. With Mom by my side and my dad so far ahead, I felt my nose sting and tears stream down my face.

Feelings hit my head like hammers. They were shoved down my throat by the heartbreaking reality right in front of me. The stark contrast between the warm embrace of the three of us in the past and the cold silence among us now pierced right through my heart.

The walk to the car was awkward and hectic. It only got worse when I stepped into the car and realized the drive would be more unbearable. As usual, I was sitting in the passenger seat in front with Dad, and Mom was sitting in the back seat. It saddened me to feel so far away from my parents when we shared the same space.

For the first fifteen minutes, no one spoke a word, yet I desperately hoped for any reactions.

They were supposed to be thrilled to see me again after months like they used to be, I thought to myself. The silence suffocated me.

To distract myself from the stifling silence around me, I aimlessly stared out of the window, watching cars and trees passing by. Grey seemed to be the dominant color, with black and white spreading across the city. December in Beijing was especially murky, with heavy traffic and sunless days. I knew the sun was out there, just above all the layers of dark clouds blocking everyone from seeing the light. The way the city was engulfed by the depressing and endless dreariness reflected the way I was trapped in this cold and ominous silence.

Finally, I could not endure the choking silence anymore and broke the breathless air. "Hmm... the winter in Beijing is just as dismal as the last time I was here."

And there went nothing.

After a minute or two, my dad said, while eyes fixed on the road ahead, "It has been getting better. The pollution is not as bad as it was."

How interesting. I thought to myself. *Months later, all my dad and I could do was chat about the weather.* We both knew the gibberish was our last line of defense before talking about the elephant in the room, which I believed neither of us wanted to start. Everyone in the car seemed to brace themselves, trying vigilantly not to step on the bomb.

"Honey, are you hungry? What do you want to eat?" That was my typical mom who usually put me first.

What seemed to be an easy question, as it used to be, became incredibly hard to answer. *Am I hungry? Yes. But should I say that though? If I say yes, that means we will be sitting around a table facing each other and any subtle facial expressions would have nowhere to hide.*

"Urr... I think we could figure out something quick at home?" I murmured, battling my precautions and doubts.

"Great! I'll cook your favorite beef stew." Mom could not help but respond with enthusiasm like always. Nothing would change her love for me.

Dad did not say a thing.

Another wave of silence filled up the space, leaving me racing to find something to say.

Usually, conversations with my dad were challenging. I always felt the need to provide a wonderful report like giving a briefing to my boss. Not a single mistake was allowed. This almost religious pressure to perform, or to strive for his approval, stems from my long-time fear of his temper since I was an infant. Dad always had a hot temper, but it worsened over time and even became volcanic.

There were so many traumatic memories of him erupting this violent fury out of nowhere, and at times, out of nothing. The monstrous look on his face when he exploded at Mom and I left a deep cut in my soul. His nasty cursing and acerbic humiliations were like acid rain pouring down on me, eroding my self-esteem and leaving scathing pain in my memories.

Finally, I saw my home at the end of the road. It still looked the same: the pebble path in the front yard leading to the front door, a piece of iron art; off the pebble path were lush roses, peach trees, pear trees, and all my favorite garden flora; surrounding the three-story house was a stream of landscape water with colorful goldfish swimming across white and violet water lilies. Everything looked the same, yet everything felt different. The house was oozing a cold, sad, and empty vibe—the joyful and loving family in the good old days was long gone. I am sure when I was away, so many heartbreaking days had passed that I could not possibly imagine what this house had witnessed.

Dad rushed ahead of Mom and I again and stormed into the house. Mom and I paced ourselves into the living room. Then the suffocating awkwardness and silence occupied the space again.

"I am heading to the kitchen to prepare the beef stew," Mom said, escaping from the stifling atmosphere, at least for a moment.

Dad and I sat on the opposite sides of the tea table, waiting out the time, with nothing to say to each other. After a while, he stood up and went to the kitchen. What happened next would forever leave a gruesome wound in my heart.

An ear-splitting clashing of pans and pots exploded from the kitchen like an earthquake. Then a flurry of glass-breaking sounds mixed with Dad's hysteric roaring like a lunatic monster. Suppressing my compounding fears, I tiptoed my way toward the kitchen.

"What--?" Wanting to ask what was going on, what I saw in front of me forced my words back. My mouth was wide open, but I could not say a thing. My eyes were crystal clear, yet I could not believe what I saw.

Dad threw glass salt bottles and kitchenware at my mom, yelling with his amorphous face, "You #%&*! How dare you say no more salt for me? Huh? You pig! F*ck you!"

The kitchen turned into a war zone, although there was only attack, no defense. My mom and I were defenseless. Dad forced Mom into a corner by the lightened stove. Mom was shivering, with her head down, flooded with shame, tears blurring her face. Sharp glass shards scattered all around, turning the once love-filled family space into a toxic, dangerous, and atrocious hell.

My mom and I were once again subdued by my dad's violent temper, but this time was different.

He hit my mom.

At that moment, I felt so small, the way I always felt in front of my dad—powerless and vulnerable. I was frozen by this horrifying scene.

As paralyzed and agonized as I was, I could still process one thing in my head. I swore to myself that one day, when I grew strong and powerful enough, I would save my mom and I from this living hell.

I had no idea how much time passed by when I could feel my own body again. A surge of impulse to escape was boiling in my blood. I wanted to run as fast and far as I could, away from this crushing horror. However, I could escape to nowhere. As big as Beijing was, I could not seek shelter anywhere else other than my own home. Grandma's place was an option, except it was 10:00 p.m. and her house was on the other side of town.

My own room was the only place I could lock myself up, shielding myself from the grueling wound bleeding my house. Perhaps the misery was too shocking and too real for me to take in. Tears had not streamed down my face this whole time until I suddenly collapsed and realized my house no longer felt like home.

CHAPTER 11

It's Time to Take off and Fly Away

———

Winter 2016 in Beijing ended like a nightmare, and spring 2017 brought me back to Atlanta—a new semester and hopefully a fresh start.

I was physically separated from my family, but my thoughts persistently lingered on the unsolved problem: my broken home. The only refuge to which I could return and seek solace was taken away by the storm of my parents' divorce. My heart sank every day, but I did not have a cure, and my home, which usually welcomed me with an open door, no longer made me feel safe.

After witnessing the horrid scene of my dad's violence, I experienced gut-wrenching torture that hit me like a ton of bricks. The dependable and adoring father I used to know changed so much I did not recognize him anymore. My new reality gave me a painful reminder that the loving family I used to have as a child was no longer there.

My Facebook feeds were flooded by my friends' posts and pictures about pleasant tropical family vacations on the islands. Their photos of feeding parrots in the rainforest or sipping coconuts by the pink-sand beach reminded me of the dreamy month I spent with my parents in Bali when I was twelve. Those merry family gatherings felt so distant.

The glamorous photos of my friends' families were a sharp contrast to the wrinkled and torn family photos that I destroyed when my mom gave me the news of my parents' divorce. My friends' elaborate Facebook posts about their love-filled family vacations suddenly became offensive, as if they were mocking my broken family and my lonely self. Photos of them cuddling up with their parents by a bonfire stabbed me right through my heart, painfully reminding me of my loss.

When I held a bowl of lukewarm ramen in my hand for a quick lunch in between lectures, I remembered Mom's words.

"Every good dish starts with a solid base, a key lesson applicable to many things in life." She often reiterated these words of wisdom when she cooked noodles for me at home.

My home and family were the foundation of my happiness, beliefs, and security, like an idiom in Mandarin conveys, "家和万事兴。(Everything in life prospers when the family is in harmony.)" When the foundation was shattered, everything in my life fell apart. The steadfast belief system I had valued since I was born was suddenly challenged by the series of unfortunate events over the past couple of years. Literature and movies made me believe in the kind of love that defies the test of time and lasts until death.

Now I realized life wasn't like what is depicted in the media. I had undergone growth and maturity since my mom broke the news of my parents' divorce. Days and months of intense meditations about loss, family, and love made me understand I was no longer the artless and ingenuous college freshman. My experiences were much more complex than I thought; they were influenced by uncertainties and shaped by my upbringing. I was simply unaware of this knowledge previously.

Just as I had suffered when I was stuck in the hospital battling pneumonia, I felt just as powerless and hurting while missing home. I lost something I could not replace. Many questions started mushrooming in my head: Why did this happen to my family? Where do I belong now? Where can I feel happy again?

I shut myself off from the world as I mourned the family I used to have during the period of bereavement. To me, grieving for a living person was such a novel concept. I was grieving for my father, who had ruined my mom's trust and mine. Even my best friends like Asma did not know where I was since I had been ignoring any texts or calls and trying to find a way to survive in my overwhelming new reality.

Professors also noticed my lack of energy and growing absence in class. After an early afternoon Italian Memoir class, Professor Ristaino invited me to her office to have a chat.

"Mary, dimmi tutto (tell me everything), what is going on?" She sat next to me and looked concerned.

"Nothing." I gave her a perfunctory response with my eyes fixating on the floor to avoid her gaze.

"Well, you used to be super energetic and proactive in class, but I noticed that lately, something has changed," Professor Ristaino said quietly and attentively.

I did not immediately respond but played with my fingers. The moment was very emotional as I debated whether to tell my professor the truth or not. Words were on the tip of my tongue, but it took courage to choose to be vulnerable, especially when I found it challenging to trust again. However, Professor Ristaino's patience and thoughtfulness made me feel comfortable with being genuine.

After about five minutes of silence, I lifted my head, looked her in the eyes, and said, "Nothing is working. My parents are divorced, and I don't know what to do."

Then I broke out into tears. I was sobbing so hard I could not continue talking.

Professor Ristaino reached out and wrapped her arms around me, and I leaned on her shoulder. She did not say anything but let me express my anguish without reservation.

When I composed myself, she said, "Sono così dispiaciuto, bellissima. (I'm so sorry, dear.) Mary, I want to support you through this difficult time."

Words could not describe how much I appreciated Professor Ristaino's empathy and heartwarming care. Maybe all this time when I kept my misery to myself, I needed someone who could listen and understand. She was one of the few professors who showed me personal attention and solicitude instead of accusing me of decreasing in my academic performance.

Other faculty members suggested I try counseling, but I was too mentally occupied and drained to retell my story to a complete stranger. Living my trauma once was enough. Besides, the ordeal made me cynical. I felt apprehension in sharing my experience with someone who did not know me at all. How would this random person help me solve *my* problems?

My cynicism pushed me to take matters into my own hands and to find answers to my questions.

Before I left Professor Ristaino's office, she said, "I know it's hard, but I think writing can be one of your ways to heal. Putting your stories and emotions on paper would help you get it all off your chest and move forward. Maybe you can't find your answers by being stuck in the past."

I thanked her again for listening and being there for me. Her advice elicited my reflection. It was so powerful I could sense my life was about to transition into a new phase. For the past few months, I had refused to let go of what happened that was beyond my control, as if I reached a dead end. Days fleeted by with my same mentality and set of destructive emotions—despair, anger, sadness, and jealousy.

Professor Ristaino inspired me to lift my head and look forward. I did not realize I was trapped in a downward spiral and needed to look in a different direction to find a way out.

I realized the answers to my questions might be in front of me, not behind me. With her words in mind, I walked back to my dorm room and opened a new journal. On the first page, I wrote:

You can't find your answers by being stuck in the past.

***

Over spring break, with my journal, I decided to escape to Savannah, an artsy coastal town about a four-hour drive away from Atlanta. The two-week excursion was my attempt to pull myself out of my continuous melancholy.

Springtime in Savannah was breathtaking. Masses of azaleas bloomed fiercely and covered the streets like carpets. Fuchsia pink camellias punctuated the gardens randomly. The floral redolence filled my nostrils—sweet, intense, and soothing. The spring breeze ran through my hair and the sun shone on my cheeks as I indulged myself in its forgiving warmth. It naturally lightened up my mood.

I took a stroll around the historic district and noticed artists spontaneously set up easels under leafy trees and start painting the scenic street corners or portraits of young couples. Violinists, jazz drummers, and singers assembled their band and played their original music pieces that captivated passersby. I could not resist but join the group of people who circled the band listening to the melodies, some dancing to the beat.

The arts had a magic power in healing. When I enjoyed myself among the crowds, my mind focused on the pure pleasure the music brought me. Dancing with the rhythm also allowed me to shake off the worries and stress that had been bogging me down for months. The refreshing tunes took me to another place where I could feel blissful and appreciate the present.

After stopping by the band, I had no clue where I should head next. The moment I felt anxious about the uncertainty ahead of me, I harkened back to a quote my parents used to teach me when I felt disoriented and fearful of the unknown.

善行无辙迹，善言无瑕谪。 *(A good traveler has no fixed plans, and is not intent on arriving.)*"

—老子 LAO TZU[5]

5   Laozi, *Tao Te Ching*, Translated by Gia-fu Feng and Jane English, New York: Vintage Books, 1972.

With the quote in mind, I wandered into the neighborhood confidently and leisurely and came across a cozy tea spot, Gryphon Tea Room. It was early afternoon, so I felt it would be perfect to ponder my questions and feel my emotions over a pot of Earl Gray or jasmine green tea.

The tearoom looked like a mini library; chairs and a couch were placed by the bookshelves, with dim lights all around. I found a seat next to a grand piano by the window. A few other guests scattered across the room, sipping their lazy and sunny afternoon away. They had friends or family to keep them company, but I was all alone.

I ordered the high tea for one and nibbled on my scones and mini salmon sandwiches. From a bookshelf adjacent to my couch, I selected a coffee table book that included a collection of aesthetic pictures of Savannah. As the hot lavender Earl Grey dissolved in my mouth, I paced myself through the photos and learned about the curious history and ghost stories that were popular with the locals.

A couple in their mid-forties entered the tearoom holding hands and sat next to my table. They had cheery smiles on their faces. When the man went to the bathroom, the lady locked eyes with me and engaged in some small talk. "Are you having tea all by yourself?"

"Yes."

"No boyfriend?"

"Nope."

She looked amazed, and said, "So traveling on your own? Good for you! How do you like Savannah so far?"

"Haha, thanks! It's a gorgeous place."

"Yeah, that's probably why so many couples visit here during springtime. Why are you traveling alone?"

I hesitated to tell her my personal story, so I said, "Soul searching. Spending some time by myself to clear my mind. I think traveling alone also allows me to pay attention to the little moments that I would not be able to appreciate with a group of loud college friends."

"Haha, you are funny. That's great."

"What are you going to order?" I asked.

"Maybe I'll start with a lobster bisque."

"Yum!"

"I love lobster and can only *hope* my husband is a lobster too."

"That's an interesting thought. Why?"

"Oh, because lobsters only stick with their one partner for their whole life," she explained before a server attended her table.

She can only hope her husband is faithful? Does she not know, or is she also dealing with betrayal? She looked happy with her husband though. I tried to digest what I'd just heard.

After I finished the last bite of my tea sweets, I left the tearoom and walked back to my hotel room. I thought more about my brief chat with the lady. Nothing was what it seemed. Her worries were hidden beneath her cheerful grin.

I could not help but contemplate my friends' Facebook family photos. The posts might not tell the truth about what was really going on. Knowing that appearance might not reflect reality inspired me to have more compassion. I never knew what people were going through and kindness could be the key to save someone's day, like Professor Ristaino did for me. My jealousy and anger faded away and were replaced by sympathy, which made me realize many people were on their healing journey. I was *not* alone.

When I returned to my hotel room, I pulled out my journal to write my thoughts on the blank pages. Words started to form into stories like jewels collected in my treasure box. By the end of my writing, it occurred to me that my trip to Savannah opened up the opportunity for me to have new encounters and gather fresh perspectives about my struggles.

Professor Ristaino was right; I would not find my answers by being stuck in the past. I had to break away and find my answers in the present, even if that meant I had to discover them in a new place. A positive feeling of hope inspired me to think about regaining control of my life instead of incessantly feeling lost and depressed.

An epiphany came to me and planted a seed in my heart, so I added a few more lines in my journal:

I am going on a pilgrimage around the world to search for home and find my answers. My healing journey starts now.

CHAPTER 12

My Heart Takes Me to Dubai

———

I pulled out a world map and tried to decide where to visit first, like a couple of summers ago when I decided to go to Israel.

The busy spring semester in my sophomore year helped me forget about the painful visit to my family during winter. A few months later, the vibrant summertime triggered my wanderlust. One thing I knew for sure—I did not want to return home, which I barely recognized and where I felt miserable.

Usually, I would do extensive research about my destination. However, this time, I let my heart take me wherever I might end up.

I found myself curious about the Burj Al Arab ("the Tower of Arab"), reportedly the world's only seven-star hotel, so I chose Dubai. I first learned about Burj Al Arab while working on an art project in primary school. My art teacher asked the students to design a creative piece of architecture. I turned to the internet to look for some of the most creatively designed architectures in the world for inspiration. Burj Al Arab caught my eye because of its statement design. It stood out in the Dubai skyline, or in a way, defined it. The silhouette of the hotel resembled the sail of a boat, which I later learned was called a dhow—an Arabian water vessel. It sat on an artificial island off Jumeirah Beach, looking like a sturdy boat ready to set sail into the ocean of wonders and unknowns.

So on a late-night flight in early June 2017, I headed to Dubai with the thought of seeing the treasure with my own eyes.

Right before we were about the land, in midair, the silhouette of Burj Al Arab stood out in the middle of the ocean, away from the cluster of skyscrapers. I was so excited I rubbed my eyes twice to absorb the sacred and majestic view.

My first impression of Dubai was that it combined modern sophistication and luxury. It was hard not to indulge in the hub of ultra-modernism. While I was looking out of the car window in transit to my hotel, the forest of skyscrapers was on full display before me. The skyscrapers defied the concept of sky, as they might well be among the clouds already. The shapes of the buildings were abstract like modern art. Shopping centers were abundant, and it was not hard to spot a fleet of Rolls Royces or Ferraris roaring on the street. It was heaven for people who needed some retail therapy.

When I stepped inside Burj Al Arab, the definition of ultimate luxury became instantly clear to me. The sky-high atrium demystified my long-standing question about how the architecture lasted with a sail-shaped exterior. Centered in the lobby was a wall of fountains. The jets and lights danced with the rhythm of the music. Gold trimmed staircases spiraled up toward the higher level where the luxury boutiques were located. Gold was the color scheme around the whole space, punctuated with royal blue to echo the vibe of the ocean. Every detail and corner of Burj Al Arab looked like a fairy tale come true. Nothing seemed impossible in this place.

As a solo traveler, I knew when visiting a place where I had never been to, a concierge would be my best friend. My concierge planned a few places for me to visit outside of the secluded tower.

Over the next few days, I strolled through the market at the Creek and Old Dubai. The neighborhood was made of one-story buildings clustered together. The dark orange walls and the busy crowds rushing to the market made the setting look like a classic movie. Over a visit to the coffee museum around the Al Fahidi historical neighborhood, some locals encouraged me to try on Jalabeya, a traditional long-sleeved dress, full-length so that it could cover my ankles. On top of the Jalabeya, I was wrapped with an abaya, a breezy, long, black coat. My outfit was finished with a shayla, a black scarf that draped over my head and covered my mouth and cheeks. I had a hard time recognizing myself in the mirror yet was stunned by my mysterious appearance.

A few locals gestured toward me to learn to dance with them. I followed their steps, and we formed an impromptu dance performance on the street. Though I didn't understand the lyrics, I shared in the lively vibe of the dancing crowd. Sweat drenched my outfit because of the torrid heat and layers of garments on my body. However, at that moment, all I cared about was dancing merrily like no one was watching. The shared joy of dancing brought me closer to the locals regardless of my language barrier. That feeling of closeness and shared joy in a historical district was the magic of Dubai for me. Among the skyscrapers, there still existed a thriving community where people embraced their cultural traditions. The Old and the New meshed together to bring out the fascinating colors of Dubai.

One successful adventure prompted me to unlock my next excursion. I found my way up to the top of the tallest building in the world, Burj Khalifa. When I looked down from the zenith, all of Dubai looked like it was under a kaleidoscope. Buildings, people, and cars were no longer objects but little color blocks clustered together. The view reminded me of the importance of zooming out. When I was on the top of the world, every nuance beneath was part of a larger and mightier ecosystem. I applied similar logic to my own life. I realized if I could see past the worries and the struggles I faced on a daily basis and stand above them, I had a chance of regaining my sense of a larger direction and purpose.

Out of the concrete jungle, my heart took me to the desert. While I was on a desert safari, I made some new friends along the way who were also solo travelers like me. Samantha, who was a couple of years older than me, had traveled to Dubai from Australia. We quickly became friends because we were the youngest among the group of travelers. The two of us ended up going sand surfing later that week.

While we enjoyed the fun of speeding through the sand, the only thing I could think of was to make the moment last a little longer. There was nothing around other than hills of gold sand shimmering in the blazing sun. An expansive and unencumbered setting usually made me feel as if I was the only human in the universe. At that moment, there was only me and the world. I felt closer to myself. A voice in my head said happiness was right in front of me.

When the sun disappeared below the horizon, the moon and stars appeared in the sky. Our group of travelers gathered around a bonfire, and a couple of locals joined us to smoke some hookah. We lost ourselves in the enchanting aroma of rose and eucalyptus and the millions of stars glowing in the dark night sky. Our slow conversations centered around the idea of simple happiness in life. We realized it did not take much for us to be so happy—a desert, a group of new friends we met along the way, a dark sky lit up by stars that shone like diamonds, and a bonfire. At that moment, we shared the gratitude for having known each other in the middle of the desert. We did not know what would happen tomorrow, but it did not matter. All we cared about was living life to the full in the present.

The vibe I felt in the desert concluded my memories in Dubai. This magical amalgam of old and new, wilderness and civilization, restored my energy to embrace the present and anticipate an even more exciting adventure the next day. When my flight to Milan took off from the Dubai International Airport, I took a glimpse of Dubai once again, and whispered, "Until next time!"

CHAPTER 13

Stumbling Upon Home in Italy

———

"Italy will never be a normal country. Because Italy is Italy. If we were a normal country, we wouldn't have Rome. We wouldn't have Florence. We wouldn't have the marvel that is Venice."
—MATTEO RENZI, PRIME MINISTER OF ITALY

Taking a walk on a random street in Rome felt like traveling through a history book. It is a city frozen in time. What better place than Rome to lose my way during my journey to find home?

In summer 2017, I was totally lost in the streets on my way to Scalinata di Trinità dei Monti. At a time when I needed Google Maps the most, my phone inconveniently died.

Tourists flooded the narrow streets weaving the tight-knit neighborhoods in Rome. My anxiety started to build up when I could not read the street signs and spoke broken Italian, all the while being pushed in an unknown direction. It was stressful to constantly try to find out where I was while staying vigilant about my surroundings to avoid dangers such as thefts or robberies.

A squad of ladies in their thirties was passing by, and I walked up to them to ask for help.

"Scusa mi... Sono totalmente...errr...persa. (Excuse me. I am totally lost.)"

I felt like a complete idiot standing in the middle of the street. The scorching sun shone on me like a giant spotlight, amplifying my awkwardness as a clueless tourist. Sweat dripped down my cheeks, and my anxiety was spilling over and screaming my incompatible existence as an outsider.

"Mah...Siamo persi come te! (Uh...We are lost like you!)" One of the ladies responded with a playful smile. She was tall and slim like an Italian supermodel. Her long, wavy hair was glowing dark hazelnut brown in the sun. She wore a chic corset-inspired rose gold crop top, a maxi ivory cotton skirt, and a pair of slick white sandals. Her look was finished with cat-eye ivory-framed shades, an oversized white beach hat, and pepper red lips. I was stunned by her beauty and enamored by her intense rose-scented perfume. More importantly, her humor calmed me down instantly and warmed my heart. She made me feel included in a strange place where I knew no one and could not feel more foreign.

"Haha! Come ti chiami? (What's your name?)" I laughed as my stressed eased and I let down my guard.

"Giana. E tu?" She was smiling while I tried my best to keep up with the conversation.

"Mary. Sei Bellissima!" I complimented her stunning look.

"Grazie! Dove stavi cercando di andare?" She asked where I wanted to go.

"Oh! Piazza Trinità dei Monti." The name of my destination popped out of my mouth.

"Ah! Okay. Why don't you join us? We'll give you the best tour in Rome," another lady of the group said to me in English with a strong yet lovely accent.

"Oh, that'll be awesome!" I hollered with excitement and could not believe my day tour in Rome started like that, with four strangers I just met on the street.

Around evening time, Giana took me back to her mom's house for dinner.

"Benvenuta, bella!" Giana's mom greeted me with a warm hug and a very Italian enthusiasm.

"Grazie mille!" I responded with the limited expressions I knew.

Giana's mom reminded me of my grandma. She always had a soothing smile on her face like the welcoming sunshine in the spring. Her eyes arched into two thin lines when she smiled like two leaves of a willow tree. She was so eager to chat with me even though most of the time I was guessing what she was saying from her expressions and gestures.

That night I had an authentic Italian family dinner. Giana's mom cooked the famous Roman pasta, *cacio e pepe*, that she was so proud of. Her beaming smile when she touted her flawless cooking skills was priceless. I sat at the round dinner table with Giana and her family, feeling at home. When I took a bite of the steamy pasta, it not only warmed my stomach but also my heart, just like the Italian family made me feel.

To this day, I am still touched by the immense hospitality of Giana's family. The ancient buildings and sites I had seen that day were amazing, but the warm welcoming of Giana's family was the most magical part of Rome. I still cannot believe how losing my way in Rome turned into having a family dinner with total strangers who made me feel at home. Giana's family made me realize that home is where you invite people in, even if it means a total stranger from the other side of the world who cluelessly lost her way in Rome.

The yearning for connection breaks the barrier of language, culture, or distance. It reminds me of home in its purest form, where family gets together and builds heartfelt and warm memories. Those memories always help you find your way home when you are lost.

***

Two weeks of my time in Italy had flown by since I first landed at Malpensa Airport. Like a feather carried away by the breeze in mid-air, somehow, I found myself in Florence. Why not?

One evening, my meandering soul took me out on the street to watch a drama show. The setting was at Palazzo Pitti, claimed by the emcee as an iconic landmark where royals used to host social gatherings. The secluded courtyard had high walls that stood tall on all four sides. The city outside seemed to be in a different world. I looked up into the night sky above me and saw stars twinkling and a moon risen high in the sky.

I found myself a seat. Enthused locals chatted diligently with their friends. I could not understand any of their conversations, so I felt out of place and did not know what to do in the short two minutes before the show. A few families sat around me, and the parents held the brochure of the show and explained it to their kids. I reminisced on when my parents took me to see the opera *Carmen*—Dad got me a tin of icy Coke and Mom walked through the opera description on the brochure with me. A kid's shriek pulled my thoughts back to the courtyard. The preshow was still lively, but I was all alone.

As the show started, the audience was taken into a different era in Italy: the Medici era. Actors and actresses dazzled the crowds with their extravagant outfits. The gold sheen on their costumes bounced off the stage lights with colors of all sorts—merlot, violet, or vermillion, all projected on my face. Sequins sparked across their bodies and overwhelmed the audience with the opulent display, which echoed the opulent period the play aimed to portray.

The show did not make much sense to me because most of the time, I could not understand a thing. Throughout the three hours, I did, however, manage to appreciate the setup and the actors' gestures and facial expressions. Under the same stars, I learned to be entertained by the musical with the locals.

Toward the ending, the girl sitting next to me unexpectedly said, "Hey! I saw you enjoyed the show quite a bit. My name is Elena. What's your name?"

"Mary! Nice to meet you. I didn't know you speak English." I was happy someone could keep me company.

"I'm a college student, and my family lives just a few blocks away." Elena had hazelnut brown hair down to her shoulders. She seemed so enthusiastic to chat with me.

"You know, I'd love to show you around the city if you are free tomorrow. Tonight, I need to get back home to have dinner with my parents."

"Wow, I'd love to. But I'm unfortunately leaving early tomorrow morning." I sighed grudgingly. Elena was probably my only chance of feeling oriented in a place where I knew no one. It was disappointing not to be able to take her up on her offer of a guided tour. Walking around with her eased my anxiety of always being on guard for potential danger.

"It's so nice to meet you, though. I hope you come back and visit. Maybe we'll bump into each other again."

We said goodbye and I lost myself in the dark night again. At first, I tried to get a cab, but there were no taxis in sight and I could not connect to the internet. My only option was walking back to my hotel.

I moved swiftly on the street so no one would follow me or think I was lost. However, after I crossed the famous Ponte Vecchio, a local guy came up to me and asked me if I wanted a photo in broken English.

At first, I felt uneasy. It was around 10:00 p.m. and I knew I should not be out all by myself. Somehow, I did not trust my instinct. I needed to leave early in the morning, which meant I might not have a chance to take a photo with the landmark, so I was tempted to accept his offer. *What would he do anyway? Many people are walking by.* So I thought.

The moment when I was about to accept his offer, two girls walked up to me and said, "Hey, where have you been all this time? We need to go watch the movie, remember?"

I looked at them, puzzled. Then they winked at me and I realized they were trying to alert me of potential danger. I quickly collected my thoughts and said, "My bad! Let's go!"

I joined the two girls and hastened away from the guy.

"What were you thinking, girl? It's very dangerous to walk alone and especially chat with a guy." They stared at me, silently accusing me of my naiveté. "We've heard many assault cases around the area, especially targeting female tourists."

"I... I don't know. I guess I didn't pay attention."

"You should really be careful! Where's your hotel? We will walk you there." They insisted on making sure I got back safely.

"Thank you so much for looking out for me. I could not imagine what would have happened if..." The more I thought about what had just happened, the more I felt chilled to the bone regarding all the ways things could have gone wrong.

"No problem. We are from Florida, also tourists. So we understand and thought we really need to look out for one another."

Their random act of kindness made me feel grateful, and their reminder was a wake-up call for me as a solo female traveler. I was lucky!

When I arrived at my hotel, they disappeared into the night. I thought to myself, Elena was certainly not representative of all the locals. It was tempting to try to befriend the locals when I felt out of place. Because of the pain I felt from my parents' divorce, I was desperate to find trust in even strangers, though my blind faith in random kindness almost got me into trouble. Believing that locals were all good-hearted and amiable was not a smart judgment every time.

***

The first time I saw Venice was in a high school art history class. We were analyzing Edouard Manet's impressionist painting, *The Grand Canal (Blue Venice)*.[6] In the painting, the water surface looked like a mosaic of mirrors that projected different shades of blue. The gondola in the painting appeared to be slowly drifting along the canal. I don't remember all of the technical details we analyzed from the masterpiece, other than the agitated surface and broken brushstrokes that reflected Manet's own restless emotions. What has stayed with me, though, was the beauty of Venice, which was waiting for me to explore.

During my trip through Italy, I found myself sitting in a gondola drifting down the Grand Canal in Venice. A local stood at the very front of the gondola, ready to steer the gondola around the other boats when we passed under a narrow bridge. He was a tall, well-tanned guy, wearing a large straw hat that blocked most of the sunshine.

While we were drifting toward a less crowded area in the canal, the gondolier started singing his favorite serenade. His voice was deep and engaging. *Wow, is it true any random Italian could sing like Andrea Bocelli?* I thought.

I noticed the dreamy water was just like Manet painted it, the shimmering sunlight dancing with the ripples. As we propelled forward in the gondola, the view of Venice unfolded in front of me. Above the blanket of water that stretched out into the distance, the silhouette of the floating city was punctuated by bridges that connected different parts of the city.

6   Edouard Manet, *The Grand Canal of Venice (Blue Venice)*, 1875, oil on canvas, 54 x 65 cm, Shelburne Museum, Shelburne.

Venice was busy during the day. The current of the crowds flowed with the current of the water. Especially during the summer, when tourists from around the world came to visit Venice, the flood of crowds seemed to be able to crush the ancient bridges at any time.

When I hopped off the gondola, I followed the crowds into whatever direction the current of people flowed. It was sometimes overwhelming to walk solo in an overpacked city in the scorching sun. I'd say Manet's paintings captured most of the beauty of Venice, but he missed one important detail— how many tourists were all around!

After struggling to find my way amid a sea of people, my body started to tell me to march to a secluded place. So I ventured into the other side of the grand canal, where my hotel was located. When the crowds started to quiet down, I realized that was where the locals lived. Their houses were tucked in by the water, along different streets.

During the day, I usually hid somewhere away from the tourists. At nighttime, I saw families go to local pizzerias to have some steamy buffalo mozzarella pizza with beer or sparkling water. One night, I tried out the local pizzeria by the river as well. The pizza definitely tasted homey, but the only thing missing was that I had no family to share it with. While I was munching on a slice of pizza, homesickness suddenly overwhelmed my senses and stung me like a bee. Tears welled up in my eyes. The view in front of me started to look like Manet's impressionist painting, in which objects became blurry and dreamy.

A server came over to my table. "What does not make you happy, miss? Something wrong with the food that upsets you so much?"

My mood was instantly lifted by his humor. I tried to push back my homesickness and smiled at him. "Tutto bene! (Everything is fine!)"

"Miss, I am sure of one thing. In Italy, we have a saying, 'nothing can't be resolved over biscuits and wine.'" He gave me a bright smile.

"How to say it in Italian?"

"Tutto finisce a tarallucci e vino," He explained. Then he disappeared before I could ask what dessert options they had.

A couple of minutes later, he brought a glass of red wine with some biscuits. I was pleasantly surprised and said, "Grazie mille! (Thanks a million!)"

I took a sip of the wine and let it melt on my tongue. While I enjoyed the mellow sensation, the homesickness also melted with the wine. I started nibbling the biscuits. Their crunchiness coupled with the mellow taste of the wine brought me so much joy and satisfaction. When I looked across the water again, the moon started to rise in the dark night. Though I was all alone in a totally unfamiliar place, at least there was a nice server who made my life a little sweeter.

That feeling of happiness and gratitude summed up my travel in Italy. Whenever I found beautiful moments in Italy, from the people I met or the places I visited, the confusion, sadness, and anguish I had been feeling about my own broken family no longer weighed me down. Italy made me believe that even though I could not see the future, my life would get better. Happiness was around me if I paid attention.

Italy also made me realize that home is not constrained to a location but can be wherever I travel. Family can even be total strangers who wanted me to feel at home, like the lovely Italian grandma who fed me *cacio e pepe*, or the server who cheered me up with *tarallucci e vino*.

CHAPTER 14

Swiss Escape

—

My heart was soaring with the birds among the clouds. Outside my window, I could see them gliding in mid-air as the mountains receded from view. My train dashed through the gorgeous landscape, like a horse galloping, as my eyes stayed glued to the scene and my mind drifted away.

I took an early morning train to Zermatt. The night before, I was still in the Italian city of Como. In fact, I did not even book my round-trip train ticket until almost 2:00 a.m.

The seven-and-a-half-hour train ride gave me abundant time to let my mind drift away and felt particularly liberating. I was free from my worries as the train dashed through the mountains.

Maybe it was because the lush greens and the crystal-clear sky outside turned me into a desperate romantic, but somehow, traces of my parents' past loving moments flashed before my eyes.

I recalled that over a family vacation when I was three years old, my parents said Grandma would take me to play for a while. I looked up to Grandma with my big glowing eyes. "Where is Mommy and Daddy going?" I asked.

Grandma smirked at me and whispered into my ears, "It's their secret."

Grandma and I ended up building a sandcastle on the beach for the entire afternoon and evening. When we returned to the suite, we saw pillows scattered all over the floor. As a three-year-old, I assumed Mom and Dad had a fight. Years after, I finally understood that my parents needed to escape to their own wonderland.

I also remembered Dad used to surprise Mom with gifts whenever he came home from his travels. One time when he returned from South Africa, he brought back a two-carat blue diamond ring. Mom shrieked with joy when Dad put the ring on her index finger.

"Don't waste money on me!" Mom said when he showered her with the lavish gift.

Dad said, "How can I not? We are always dating, aren't we?"

Consumed with the painful thoughts of my dad's betrayal and the divorce, these loving memories had nearly vanished. I was so glad they resurfaced during my train ride to Zermatt.

When I arrived, I found myself in a serene village tucked away in the Alps. The pristine view of the forests and the water flowing into the lakes convinced me I could escape to no better spot. I quickly dropped my stuff at my hotel and started brainstorming ways to spend my time.

During my getaway in Zermatt, there were two experiences I could never forget. I paraglided from the top of the Alps and rode a horse back to the top.

I went to the top of the Alps with my instructor after finishing a glass of bubbly rosé, ready to take off. My instructor ensured that I was well harnessed with my outfit and equipment, and then he let out the parachute. We were facing the abyss from the top, and I could feel my heart racing.

"When I tell you to run as fast as you can, do what I say, ok? That way we can take off successfully," my instructor reminded me.

Though my head doubted my ability to fly, my heart was ready to take a dive. *What was the worst that could happen? I would be among the clouds anyway.* I tried to convince myself to fight off my fears.

Once my instructor found the ideal wind, he hollered for me to canter like a horse. I took off like a stallion until the point my feet were off the ground. With a thrust of fresh air pushing us upward, I spread out my arms and realized I was flying in the sky. I screamed ecstatically and enjoyed listening to my voice bouncing off among the tranquil mountains. Pieces of fluffy clouds floated around me. I could actually slide my fingers through some of the thinner and small ones. It was magical.

While I was flying, an epiphany dawned on me about healing. Every day I hoped and prayed for a happier life, away from the agonies that had been consuming me. My fear that life might not get better had been standing in the way of my happiness. This was similar to my paragliding experience. Until my feet were off the ground, my fear of falling still shackled me. I ran faster instead so I could break free from the emotional turmoil that had been consuming me.

When my feet landed on the ground again after an hour of paragliding, my mind felt light and refreshed. "This is awesome!" I opened my arms to the sky and faced the sun with my eyes closed. I felt a stream of energy run through my body, and I thought it was hope. I was ready to live without fear.

With my renewed energy, I hopped on another adventure the next day. I decided to ride a horse to the top of the mountain. The start of the ride was calm and scenic, but as I rose higher in the mountain, the road became narrower. On my right-hand side were rocks, but on the left-hand side was the cliff. If I fell from the horse on the wrong side, I would fall thousands of feet down and would not survive. The road was not only narrow but also bumpy, with scatter pebbles or rocks that could make my horse tumble. Feeling reckless, I kicked the horse harder to start a trot. The horse started cantering on the way up to the top of the mountain.

Unlike cars, horses have moods and emotions. As I was blazing up the mountain road, we reached a sharp turn. The horse bucked and turned its neck. I was thrown off balance and fell. Then everything turned black.

When I opened my eyes again, I was surprised I was still alive. I was lucky I fell on the right side and didn't roll down to the abyss of the cliff.

I tried to sit up from the ground. My horse was still next to me. I felt lightheaded, and my body was in so much pain. My lungs felt out of place because of the big fall. Blood oozed from my knees. I knew I had to stand up as fast as I could to prevent the horse from stepping on me or kicking me.

When I stood up again, I realized I had no idea what to do next. The road was too narrow for me to turn the horse around and go downhill. And there was no way I could walk down the mountain because it would take God knows how long. My only option was to get back on the same horse that threw me off and keep going up. About an hour later, my horse and I reached the zenith. The sweeping view of the fluffy clouds, verdant valleys, and icy mountaintops made the scary fall earlier all worth it.

While traveling, I always wished that, somehow, I was born in a different family, like the happy and loving families I had been seeing in the places I explored. I wished I had a family where my dad would not betray and hurt my mom and I. However, I realized, just like the situation I was in with the horse, my only choice was to do something with what I had. It was pointless to wish for something that would never happen, and something completely out of my control. After falling from a horse on the top of the Alps, I no longer wasted my time thinking about "what ifs" but tried to get back into my life with a new attitude.

After the long-weekend escape in Zermatt, I left the Alps with new perspectives on healing myself.

CHAPTER 15

Healing With Mom in Europe

The last time I saw mom was over that traumatic home visit during my winter break when Dad slapped Mom across her face with his explosive rage. After almost a year, we were finally going to reunite.

How had Mom been coping with the trauma from the divorce? What had she been thinking in her healing journey? I thought about these questions while trying to find my way out of the crowds at Piazza del Campo, a city square at the heart of Siena, to find Mom based on the location she texted me.

Mom embarked on her own healing solo travels in Italy as well and surprised me with a reunion in Siena. She had been spending two months sipping *vino* as *aperitivo*, painting under the Tuscan sun at a vineyard, and learning how to cook *Bucatini all'Amatriciana* with handsome local chefs.

Suddenly, a familiar figure appeared in my sight and I noticed Mom's face. She looked much thinner than the last time I saw her. *Did she have trouble eating?* I wondered.

I sprinted toward her and gave her a big hug. "妈妈! 我不敢相信您在这儿! (Mom! I cannot believe that you are here!)"

Mom was too overjoyed to see me to say anything. She studied me from head to toe and reached out to touch my cheeks lovingly.

Most of the crowd had disappeared, so we decided to lie on the cement square side by side and stare at the blue sky with clouds floating by.

"So how's your trip, Mom? Where have you been? What have you done?" I asked.

"Amazing! I love Italy so much. One day I have to come and study the arts. I've been to so many places. The major cities, but also some beach towns, Sicily, Napoli, Cinque Terre," she elaborated in Mandarin. "I learned how to make pasta with a local chef, did a painting of the landscape at a vineyard, and became an amateur wine connoisseur." While Mom continuously shared her cultivating memories in Italy, the warm grin on her face looked like the summer rose I found at the gardens in Isola Bella.

It was touching to see my mom so happy again. However, I did notice a trace of white hair hidden among her black silky locks. She must have felt exhausted from dealing with the emotional stress imposed by Dad.

"Sounds like you are really living the life! You certainly did more than me." I could not help but feel happy for Mom.

Then for a while, we went silent. We simply gazed into the sky and tried to enjoy the view. I knew that the next thing we needed to let out was our shared experience in healing. The topic was heavy, and we both needed time to process.

"So, how have you been? I mean, how are you feeling?" Mom turned her head toward me and gazed at me.

"I'm... So much has happened. At first, I felt lost, angry, and sad. Then I started to accept the new reality. And now I am just trying to be happy when I can," I said in a low and soft voice, trying hard to hold back my tears.

Trauma had a way of inflicting pain again whenever I revisited it. However, it seemed impossible to avoid it when I was chatting with my mom.

"It's okay to cry. You've been through a lot. I know how you feel." Mom knew me well enough to notice the tears swirling at the corner of my eyes.

"So how did you deal with everything? Don't you feel furious, sad, or even sometimes, hopeless?" I asked her.

Mom paused a bit and her eyes turned toward the sky again. She said quietly, "You know, my only hope was you. Sometimes I even thought about disappearing from the world and that was it. But I thought I could never do that because you need me."

I was shocked. *Mom thought about suicide?* I rolled over and held her in my arms tightly.

"Don't you ever say or think stupid things like that!" I demanded. "And yes, you are right. I only have one mom in this world. I thought I already lost the dad I used to know, so I could not lose you too!" Tears streamed down my face.

"Yes, we need each other. We will save each other from this too," Mom whispered.

We helped each other dry our tears and exhaled together to release our grief.

"My friends are heading home today. But hey, what do you say we have a mom-and-daughter trip in Europe?" Mom stood up and tried to pull me up. She looked cheerful and her beautiful smile showed on her face again.

"Friends?" I was not aware that Mom traveled with her friends.

"Yes! I started the trip on my own but made new friends along the way! I'm sure you can relate to that." Mom winked at me and reminded me of her sociable character.

Mom's sharing reminded me of how deeply I resonated with her therapeutic journey. Now that we reconvened, I was thrilled about the idea of exploring Europe with Mom while we were both away from home and traveling. So I jumped up from the ground and took my mom's hand, ready to start our adventure together.

***

Mom and I chose to spend a week in Paris and a few days in Amsterdam.

We were both hurt by a loved one, so we thought we would rekindle the hope of love again in the City of Lights. One long afternoon, we sat outside of Ladurée on Champs Elysees and munched on our strawberry vanilla macaroons while sipping a glass of sparkling rosé diced with red rose petals. On another sunny day, we visited the Louvre and the Palace of Versailles. One slow evening, we climbed up to the top of Arc de Triomphe and savored the sweeping view of

Paris with the blazing sunset in the background. We waited until the laser light on the top of the Eiffel Tower shot into the starry night.

Mom and I chatted about how enchanting Paris was while we were strolling along the Seine. I asked what she was looking for in love when she was younger. Mom chuckled and pinched my arm.

"I wanted what every young girl wanted. I thought love would be everything I had ever dreamed of. Just like a fairy tale. But later, you will understand when you find your relationship, it is not all that." Mom sighed and looked into the distance, lost in thought.

"What changed? I mean what do you think love is now?" I pushed Mom to finish her thought.

"Well...Why don't you tell me what you think it is?" Mom looked at me with a sly grin.

"I want this person to be adventurous. And we will travel the world together. I want it to be exciting." I started listing all the qualities I wanted in this hypothetical boyfriend.

"Like what I thought. You know when you grow up, you might one day realize, like I do now, that love is companionship. Whoever sticks to the end with you is more than enough. What else could you ask for?" Mom seemed to be pensive.

I sensed she was thinking about Dad's betrayal again.

To distract her, I reminded Mom that we had a dinner reservation at the Eiffel Tower, which pulled her back from her own world. We quickly speed-walked toward the tower. We were both excited about climbing up those stairs to earn our five-course dinner at the Michelin-starred restaurant, Jules Verne.

It was our last dinner in Paris before heading to Amsterdam.

While we climbed up the Eiffel Tower, all of Paris was in our view. Our elevation reminded me of the epiphany I had when I was on the top of Burj Khalifa, the tallest building in the world, in Dubai.

"Mom, this view reminds me of something I realized when I was on the top of the world in Dubai."

"What did you find out?" Mom stood next to me, overlooking the city.

"When we zoom out from our daily trivial problems, the thorny troubles might no longer bother us because we see a bigger picture of our life. It's like how we are viewing the city right now. You would not bother about the traffic anymore when you are here high up on the Eiffel Tower, would you?"

Gold sunrays shone on our faces. When I felt the forgiving warmth of the bright sunshine, I said to my mom, "This is pure happiness. Us together, watching Paris in the sunset high up at the Eiffel Tower."

Over dinner, while chewing the juicy escargots, Mom kept saying how much she thought I grew up. I shared with her that though solo traveling had brought me new perspectives to solving old problems, it could not compare with traveling with her. Breathtaking views seemed much more beautiful when shared with the person I love.

Mom and I reconnected with love again in Paris.

Our time in Amsterdam was not as smooth as that in Paris. Mom wanted me to take pictures of her wherever we went, whether it was at a tulip market or in front of a colorful windmill. I began getting impatient with her and refused to take any more photos for her.

"I have been taking photos of you the whole time. You are so selfish," Mom accused me scathingly.

The frustration, sadness, and fury we both felt in the past few months resurfaced, and we confronted each other. When I could not take her criticism anymore, I finally lashed out, "You know, in the past few months, I thought about how life would be much easier if I'd been born in a different family!"

The moment those words came out, my heart sunk and I knew I had made a big mistake. Mom's jaw dropped in anger and surprise, and her body began to shake. My words must have stabbed her to the heart.

"How dare you talk to me like that!" Mom raised her voice, regardless of people walking by us.

My face burned with shame. Still feeling indignant, I mumbled, "I just meant that I *thought* about it. Had I been born in a family in which my dad would not betray us, we would not have to struggle like this."

"You know sometimes I thought you'd grown up, but other times, I don't even know who you are." Mom's voice was shaking with disappointment.

She took me to a suit boutique and bought a nicely cut and well-polished suit for Dad. She said, "Regardless of what he did, your dad is your dad. What happens between him and I should not interfere with your attitude toward him."

Though I did not understand Mom's point at the time, her words did stick in my head.

"I will bring it back and just say you picked the suit for him," Mom insisted.

Before my mom's flight back to Beijing, and me heading to Emory for the fall semester, I asked her a couple of questions that had been on my mind for a long time.

"Why did you choose Dad if you knew his temper and his flaws? And why are you trying to convince me to reestablish the broken relationship between him and me?" I asked with puzzlement.

"It's all for you." Mom did not say more than that.

I reached out and gave her a warm embrace.

Then Mom said, "To me, being with you is the happiest thing I could ask for."

I watched her disappear into the crowds as she passed security and headed in the opposite direction of where I was going.

I could not forget how she said: "It's all for you." I felt grateful that Mom endured all the pain and stress of being with my dad just so I could have a family. And she still tried to reconcile the relationship between my dad and I because she wanted me to feel I still had a family, even though it was broken.

When I was on the flight to Atlanta, the time I spent with Mom in the past couple of weeks in Europe flashed in front of my eyes. Thinking about how happy she was when we were together made me want to consider trying to rebuild the broken bond I shared with my family.

After all, what would traveling mean if, at the end of the day, I had no home to which I could return?

PART 4

ALMOST HOME

"When the camera flashed, I realized that
I had not taken a new family photo in a
long time."

CHAPTER 16

Finding Love on Tinder?

In mid-August, I returned to Emory from my summer odyssey in Europe. Five countries, about fifteen cities, three islands, and a desert later, I was ready to find a place to rest, or someone to lean on.

I turned to Tinder! Casual conversations with total strangers sounded fun to me. I downloaded the app on my iPhone and created a profile.

My profile read like this: *A twenty-year-old globe-trotter who loves playing polo among other things. Talk to me about fashion, traveling, and art.*

Then I found a photo of me taken in Venice when I was on a gondola and made it my profile picture. Voila! I was ready to take on Tinder.

While swiping, one profile caught my attention for much longer than a few seconds.

Kristiaan, 24. Financial advisor. Graduated from Georgia Tech a couple of years ago. Love bubble tea. Down to stroll around the park and chat. Hobbies include hiking, archery, and having a nice conversation. I'm also a pro on back massages :P

He probably used his LinkedIn profile picture for Tinder, and his other photos were of him chilling with his cat or hiking with his friends.

Also love bubble tea! Instead of waiting for guys to make the move like many girls do, I shot a text in the chat box.

After a few seconds, he texted back. First with a smiling face. :) And then: *Oh yeah? Want to get some together?*

I replied. *Why not! Let's meet at my place at 6:00 p.m. tomorrow? 14 Eagle Row. Then we head over to grab bubble tea.*

Yay! Works perfectly because I have plenty of time to pick you up after work. See you soon tomorrow!

Just like that, we finished up our first chat.

That was a Wednesday night. Sunset had already passed and left the last few threads of purple and pink in the sky. The moon had risen in mid-sky already. Everything was quieting down, and the heat was replaced with a nice cool breeze on a late summer evening.

I was looking forward to the next day.

***

"Hey! How are you?" He looked at me from inside the car with a smile.

Kristiaan was wearing a sleek dark gray suit and yellow-striped tie. His banker look was finished with a pair of dark brown Oxford loafers. He came straight from work exactly as he promised. The only thing missing was cologne. I was usually overwhelmed by the pungent smell of expensive cologne when I was among a group of bankers, but that wasn't the case with Kristiaan.

I could tell he was tall because his driver's seat was pushed back so his legs had enough room while driving. He had well-cut dark blond hair with short bangs neatly pinned toward his right ear. His eyes were deep and glowed like dark sapphires.

"My day's been good. Sorry for running late. My meetings spilled over." I quickly slid into the car and closed the door. In fact, I felt a bit ashamed when I told him the reason why I was late. In reality, I'd forgotten about our date.

"It's all good. Don't worry about it." He started the engine and drove out of the Emory bubble.

"So what do you do exactly?" I turned my head to him and asked, slightly amused.

"I am a financial advisor at a financial services firm. The office is in Buckhead next to the Ritz Carlton. So how are you enjoying Emory?"

"People are really nice, and I really can't complain."

"Good! College days feel like a long time ago for me now." He sighed and pensively looked into the distance.

"What did you do at Tech?"

"I majored in Aerospace Engineering for freshman and sophomore year. And then I switched into double majors in Industrial Engineering and Finance." He casually spoke about engineering and his three majors as if it was all a piece of cake.

A typical Tech nerd, so I thought. And from our conversation so far, I could tell he was an introvert.

"What did you do for fun?"

"Ha! You think I studied all day? I loved hiking with friends. And I did trading for fun and paid my own tuition."

The more I got to know him, the more I realized he was more nerdy than I thought. It was thrilling and amusing to get to know a little bit more about his life by the minute.

We soon arrived at Honey Bubble, a popular bubble tea place near Ponce Market. Kristiaan parked and we went inside. He got Taro bubble tea, and I got the regular milk tea with boba. We sat down on a soft, massive couch and kept chatting.

During the first few minutes of our conversation, we discussed our parents.

"Are your parents here in Atlanta?" I asked.

"My dad is. But my mom is back in North Carolina," he said, and then put his head down and stared at his bubble tea. He seemed to be lost in thought again.

"Oh? Why are they not..." I realized the answer before I finished the question.

He looked back at me and murmured, "They were divorced when I was nine. And my little sister was only five."

"Oh, I am so sorry. You don't have to talk about it if you don't want to. I didn't mean to..." I quickly wanted to shift the topic because I knew how piercingly painful it must be for him to tear the wound open again.

"It's okay. I've grown up a lot ever since," he said in a calm and deep tone.

When he mentioned his parents' divorce, I felt instantly connected with him. Knowing he went through something similar broke my heart but also made me realize I was not alone. It dawned on me that he could offer some guidance for me.

"If you don't mind, what has it been like since then?" I asked him.

"It was nasty at the beginning. My dad had an explosive temper and at a point, was an alcoholic. My mom took me and my sister away from our house when one night my dad stormed into the house wasted. He was yelling and breaking things and almost hit me, my mom, and my sister. So my family split after that." He went silent again, and I could see the deep pain of the past resurfaced on his face.

I reached out and held one of his hands to show my support.

"Then there was a period when I was stuck in between my parents who constantly wanted me to take sides. It was hard to live with my family split up because instantly I became a caretaker for my little sister and myself," he continued.

"Hey, I think the sun is setting. Why don't we go outside?" I tried to pull him out of his traumatic memory of the past and suggested we switch the setting to get some fresh air.

"Sounds good to me!" He seemed elated.

Kristiaan took me to Piedmont Park to continue our conversation. We strolled side-by-side and followed along the trail that led us deep into the expansive greens. Among the tall and shadowing trees, cicadas sang at their peaks for the approaching summer finale. A few Canada geese drifted on the lake, taking their nap. Some people were jogging, and others were sitting on the swinging bench and marveling at the sunset.

There was nothing like seeing a sunset by the lake at Piedmont. The sky started to display its color feast of unicorn shades, a lavish fusion of rose pink, lavender, and powder blue. Kristiaan and I kept walking until we found a secret spot where we were unencumbered. I stood by the water, looking across the lake.

"What is it?" Kristiaan seemed to sense my sudden silence and my pensive look.

"Oh. It's just...My parents just got divorced not long ago. And I still feel pretty...pretty distraught. The tension and pain can never be fully healed. They keep churning and distorting my heart," I said in a shaky voice.

"Thanks for sharing that with me. You know, I understand completely." He moved closer and tried to lock eyes with me.

"I know you do. And you are actually the first person I shared it with outside of my family. Crazy isn't it? I mean we just met and barely know each other." I started to speak faster and felt puzzled by the instant bond I felt with Kristiaan.

"But I get it. Sometimes you feel better talking to a stranger than anyone who knows you," he spoke to my heart.

We kept walking around the park and finally found a bench and sat down. When Kristiaan was sitting next to me, he was like an old friend who made me feel calm. Even if things did not develop romantically, I could sense that Kristiaan could be a great friend.

By the time we finished our conversation, Kristiaan and I realized we had been together for almost four hours. It did not feel like four hours at all because we seemed to have more and more to talk about.

We exchanged numbers that night and left the rest to fate.

***

On Sunday morning, I woke up to gold sunrays shining on my cheeks through the window. I grabbed my phone on the side table and saw that it was about 11:00 a.m., and there was an unread message from Kristiaan.

What's your plan today? He asked.

Nothing planned yet.

Wanna go hiking together?

I've not thought of that but why not?!

Perfect! I'm driving to your place. Get ready in fifteen minutes. No traffic today!

While we climbed up the trail, Kristiaan and I chatted about our hobbies, our favorite movies, and the places we had been in the world. Kristiaan was especially curious about my childhood since I grew up on the other side of the world.

Before we realized it, we had talked our way up to the top of the mountain, where a beautiful waterfall streamed down into the abyss. We stood side by side, speechless and mesmerized by the sweeping view. When I lost myself in the moment, it suddenly occurred to me that the hike with

Kristiaan reminded me of all the times I went mountain climbing with Dad. The feeling of confidence and victory was so familiar to me. Somehow that moment at the summit brought me back to the happy times I used to share with my dad. I was stunned by the déjà vu.

Kristiaan leaned over and held my hands. I looked into his sapphire blue eyes that reflected the colors of the waterfall and the sky. His eyes seemed to speak his thoughts. He gazed at me longingly and then pulled me closer. After we looked at each other for a few more seconds, we both leaned forward and dived into a passionate kiss. We closed our eyes and felt each other's breath. Love ran through my body and made me feel the tingling blend of excitement, passion, and joy. The kiss felt like an eternity. I could feel both of our hearts pounding faster.

When we felt more people were reaching the overlook area, we pulled away, but our eyes were still locked on each other. I could feel my face burning with passion, and Kristiaan was blushing as well.

"Funny thing, isn't it?" I chuckled while still feeling dazzled by the kiss.

"What is?" Kristiaan looked into the distance again.

"This stupid Tinder thing. Who would've thought we...? It all started with having bubble tea together at Piedmont Park," I said.

"I believe Tinder is what you make of it." Kristiaan had the talent of constantly speaking my mind.

"Touché."

"Do you believe in fate?" he asked.

"I do. You?"

"Same," Kristiaan looked at me and said. "I think that our connection is special."

Words seemed to fall short, so we continued admiring the view together.

CHAPTER 17

My New Happy Place

In front of college dorms, moms and dads were unloading cardboards from the trunks of their cars. They lifted them upstairs to the newly refurbished rooms their children would call home for the next semester. It was the start of my junior year at Emory.

Every time I saw my peers move into their new rooms with their parents' help, I thought about my parents. I did not have the luxury of moving into my new place with their help because they were always seven thousand miles away.

Kristiaan knew about my homesickness through my occasional mental breakdowns over several late-night conversations. So he took on the role of helping me move into my new dorm at the beginning of my school year. He gently dismantled the furniture and sorted it nicely into boxes. Then he set it all up in my new happy place. Kristiaan went to IKEA or other malls to get extra decor such as paper lanterns and house plants. He even made sure the color of my curtain matched the comforter. He tried his best to make my new room as homey as possible.

I realized that Kristiaan started playing my mom's role. Had my mom had the opportunity to be with me, she would painstakingly make sure my room was well organized and decorated. "你的小窝就是你的新家。得确保一切都淘你喜欢。Your room is your new home. We have to make sure it is exactly to your liking," Mom would say.

My room was essentially my little home far away from home. I felt grateful that Kristiaan saw the importance of setting up my new dorm room to make me feel at home. He bought photo clips and string lights that glowed in the dark to display my photos on the wall. He also got me house plants to add some healthy green in my room. When I felt stressed and fatigued, I took a good look at the ivory and pearl pink orchids. The colorful and fragrant blossoms instantly made my day a bit sweeter.

On my twenty-first and twenty-second birthdays, Kristiaan helped me set up my birthday parties to celebrate with my friends and I.

April 14, 2018 was a sunny Saturday. Spring in Atlanta felt like a festivity to me. The temperature was around 65°F, warm enough for people to enjoy the outdoor sunshine and fresh air, and not so hot that people would feel dreary. Cherry blossoms painted the city in baby pink and spread their petals in the mild breeze. Tulips and camellia flowers added more colors to the spring as well, and their aroma blended into the breeze that created a natural and unique perfume.

Kristiaan reserved an area on top of Ponce City Market, the iconic landmark where locals gather for food, drinks, or shopping. He knew I loved rooftop views, so when he took me up to 9 Mile Station, the restaurant where my birthday would take place, I was overjoyed.

Over twenty of my friends came to my birthday party. Every one of them brought me thoughtful presents. Because it was my twenty-first birthday, when I unraveled the satin ribbons or dug through the vibrant gift papers, there were bottles of red wine and sparkling rosé. I also received books that spoke to my interests in entrepreneurship and women empowerment, boxes of chocolates, and many beautifully handwritten cards.

I welcomed all my friends by starting the party with a brief speech. "I have made friends with every one of you at different points in college. I am so lucky to have you in my life, to grow together and lift each other up! Enjoy my twenty-fun party!"

Kristiaan popped a bottle of champagne he prepared for me, a bottle of Veuve Clicquot Brut 2008 yellow label. "To my birthday girl!" Kristiaan hollered while he poured the sparkling champagne into crystal glasses. He handed me a glass and then raised a toast with my friends, and said, "Happy twenty-first, my love!"

It was as if it was *his* birthday because he seemed to be happier and more excited than me. His love for me was written all over his face.

Then the server brought a big Tiffany blue box to the table. I was puzzled, so I gave Kristiaan a look of surprise. He did not say anything but gave me a sly grin.

When I opened the box, an exquisite birthday cake revealed itself—a round coconut cake with chocolate icing on the top that said, "Happy twenty-first Birthday, Mary!" My favorite flavor was coconut, so I felt like I was in heaven when I saw the ample amount of coconut flakes coat the cake like ivory velvet.

I was stunned by the cake and looked at Kristiaan with so much gratitude and happiness. He took every one of my favorite things to heart, and I could see how much effort and thought he put into planning this birthday party for me.

Though Kristiaan was a few years older than all of my friends, he seemed to enjoy chatting with them to make me happy. We savored the rich and filling cake while marveling at the sweeping view of Atlanta from the top of Ponce. Fluffy clouds decorated the bright blue sky. Gold sunrays shined down on the city that was surrounded by lush greens and thriving floras.

I walked around the table toward Kristiaan, leaned in until I was close to his ear, and said, "Thank you for doing this!"

"Of course. What else am I supposed to do? I'm your boyfriend." Kristiaan winked at me.

On my twenty-second birthday, Kristiaan reserved a venue at an art studio. He knew my passion for the arts. A few of my friends celebrated with me, sipping rosé, painting some potteries, and chatting about our plans after graduation.

My parents used to always celebrate my birthdays with me. After I left for college, I missed being home on my birthday when I reminisced about the old times when Dad surprised me with gifts and Mom made me Long-Life Noodles. My birthday memories became especially painful now that my family was broken. However, when I looked at Kristiaan's loving smile on my twenty-second birthday and thought about the last birthday we celebrated together, I realized he was trying the fill the gap of my mom's presence.

Kristiaan locked eyes with me when he noticed my pensive look. He came over and asked, "Everything okay?"

"Oh yes. I was thinking about the past birthdays I had with my parents."

"I know. But are you happy right now?"

"Of course I am. I feel like you are doing what my mom would have done if she was here with me. I really cherish it." I hugged Kristiaan.

"I'm sure that I cannot match up to your mom, but I will keep trying," he said.

That evening, Kristiaan sent my mom the photos he took of me at my birthday party. He texted Mom that he was trying to make me happy and hoped he did a good job doing that. Mom called me and said she was so grateful I had Kristiaan by my side.

Though I could no longer celebrate my birthdays with the family I used to have, at least Kristiaan tried to create a new one where I felt loved at home.

***

Kristiaan and I raced to the airport. He drove over the speed limit on the highway and I sat in the passenger seat, heart pounding fast because Mom's flight was landing right about then. It was around 11:00 p.m. on May 11, 2019, one day before Mother's Day.

It had been about two years since the last time I saw Mom in Europe, where we spent some mom-and-daughter time together from Italy, France, to the Netherlands in summer 2017. This time, my mom was flying to Atlanta all the way from Beijing to attend my graduation, which would happen in two days.

"I can't believe I will see my mom again so soon!" I could not contain my excitement.

"We are well on our way. Should be at the airport in about twenty minutes." Kristiaan also seemed to be elated because it was his first time meeting my mom in person after dating me for about two years.

Mom must be so tired after seventeen hours on her flight. I started to think about how to make Mom feel as relaxed as possible after her long journey across the Pacific Ocean.

"Well, we did a good job setting up everything for Mom. Hope she could feel just at home staying with us here." Kristiaan looked a bit nervous yet confident. Mom would stay with us at Kristiaan's apartment, which was much more spacious than my dorm. Since he and I started dating, I spent every weekend with Kristiaan at his place.

Over the past few weeks or so, he made every effort to prepare for his first meeting with my mom and hoped to make his first impression as flawless as possible. Kristiaan bought a new wardrobe just for my mom so she could hang all her clothes nicely without cramming them into her luggage. He also got some new sheets because I told him Mom particularly liked soft and feathery linens. He also cleaned his apartment inside out so that everything looked clean and spotless.

Kristiaan parked his car in a spot close to the arrival pickup area. He then quickly walked to the back of his car and opened the trunk. Much to my heart's delight, it turned out that he prepared surprise gifts for mom—a bouquet of red roses and a gigantic heart-shaped balloon that said "Happy Mother's Day." Kristiaan held the bouquet with his left hand and the balloon with his right.

We sprinted toward the escalator where people anxiously stretched their necks to spot their family or friends. It was late and we both started to yawn, but Kristiaan and I had our eyes wide open. About fifteen minutes later, I spotted Mom's head rising above the escalator, and I screamed, "妈! 这边儿。 (Ma! Over here.)" Kristiaan hollered, "Mama!" as well.

When Mom first saw us, her eyes instantly got bigger and her face was filled with joy, despite a hint of exhaustion. She rushed toward Kristiaan and I and gave us a warm embrace. Words could not describe the heartfelt moment when my mom and I reunited after two years.

"我想死你啦。 (I miss you so much, sweetheart,)" Mom said softly.

"我也是! (Me too, Mom!)" I noticed my voice was shaking.

After the hug, she took a good look at Kristiaan.

"你好妈妈! 很高兴见到您! (Hello, Mom! Very happy to meet you!)" Kristiaan spoke the limited Mandarin he knew in hopes of making a good impression.

"Hello!" Mom chuckled at Kristiaan's diligent pronunciation.

"妈妈, 提前祝您母亲节快乐! (Mom, happy Mother's Day in advance!)" Kristiaan gave my mom the balloon and the roses. This time, he made a couple of mistakes in pronunciation. There are four tones in Chinese characters and Kristiaan often could not distinguish between the second and third tone.

Mom's eyes sparkled despite her sleepiness. She was thrilled by Kristiaan's gifts and gave him a big hug. She could not stop smiling. It had been a long time since I had seen Mom overjoyed without any worries clouding her beautiful smile.

"Thank you so much, my love," Mom said in Mandarin, while I translated.

We both held Mom's hands as we walked together toward the baggage claim. Kristiaan took two heavy luggage bags off the belt and rolled them along without Mom lifting a finger. Mom was so happy that she got to be with me again and finally meet my boyfriend in person.

During the car ride to Kristiaan's apartment, Mom said she had dreamed about being with me again, and she was so delighted that Kristiaan had been there for me when she could not.

"Thank you so much for taking care of my daughter!" I translated for Kristiaan.

"That's what I'm supposed to do, Mom! Thought it's part of the job description?" Kristiaan charmed her with his sense of humor.

We arrived at Kristiaan's place. The room was squeaky clean and had everything Mom needed to feel comfortable. When she went to the bedroom and saw the closet and sheets, Mom said, "Wow. Thank you for setting everything up!"

"Please make yourself feel at home," Kristiaan said, repeating the same thing he said to me when I first moved into his apartment.

"Thanks, honey." Mom sat on the bed with the soft sheets and looked around. Her eyes spoke how proud of us she felt.

"You really have grown up, Yaoyao. You know how to take care of Mom." She gave me a big pat on my back.

Kristiaan insisted Mom and I sleep together on the bed, and he would sleep on the couch in the living room. Mom was very touched by his thoughtfulness. She said before bed, "Today is one of the happiest days in my life!" Tears of joy were dripping down her cheeks. I was so happy I could make Mom feel immensely happy and proud. She deserved the world after what she had been through.

The next morning was Mother's Day! Kristiaan and I woke up before Mom, sneaked into the kitchen, and prepared breakfast for her. We cooked a big omelet with eggs, cherry tomatoes, tofu, and diced mushrooms. Kristiaan also took out a big cake he hid in the fridge and gestured for me to hold it and give it to Mom.

After we finished cooking, Kristiaan and I tiptoed our way into the bedroom, hoping to surprise Mom with breakfast in bed so she could wake up to a festive celebration.

"妈, 快起床啦! (Mom, time to wake up!)" I whispered in mom's ear. Even in her sleep, her lips were arched upward and formed a sweet smile.

Mom slowly opened her eyes, and after a few blinks, they started to glow. "Wow..." Mom could not believe what was in front of her. She sat up and took the big plate of fresh and sizzling omelet from Kristiaan. Mom was so surprised she could not speak a word but gave Kristiaan and I a big hug. When Kristiaan and I were in Mom's arms, I thought *This is the feeling of home I have been looking for this whole time.*

Home, at that moment, was not necessarily a physical location anymore. I realized it lives in the people who love me deeply. A warm feeling of love ran throughout my body and soothed the wound in my heart that had been aching for over two years. Love and happiness had felt so out of reach for me since the day I lost the home I knew. However, when I was in Mom's arms with Kristiaan, the two things I had been yearning for came back to me. The feeling of love was so powerful that I could even forgive all the days I spent alone searching for a place to belong and the nights I went to sleep in tears.

I opened the box and put the cake next to Mom. She was enjoying her omelet while amazed by the glazed dark chocolate cake. The icing on the top said, "Thanks, Mom! Happy Mother's Day!" She burst into tears of joy. I was so grateful that I had a boyfriend who put so much thought into making my mom happy, and who treated my mom just as his own.

Without the need to put our emotions into words, all three of us felt the kind of happiness that only belonged to family. After over two years of traveling solo around the world to find home, I could finally anchor my heart to the home I found on Mother's Day in my boyfriend's apartment.

CHAPTER 18

Family Photo at Graduation

Dad landed in Atlanta the night before my graduation on May 13, 2019.

It was the first time I had seen him in two years, which was when I flew back home and he had slapped Mom in the face. During the time in between, we never spoke to each other—no messages and no phone calls. In a way, I was happy Dad could witness and celebrate the conclusion of my four years at Emory; on the other hand, I felt angry—he'd been absent all this time from the role of being a responsible father, and now he chose to show up in my life again?

I was apprehensive about meeting Dad again because I had no idea how he would react. One time when I was at the airport back home, about to hop on a flight back to Atlanta for my second semester of freshman year at Emory, he threw his temper tantrum again. Usually, before I left home for a long time, my parents would send me off together and we'd have a lovely meal before I headed over to security. However, that time, Dad was pissed off again about something Mom and I said. He stormed off into the distance and disappeared from the crowds without saying goodbye. After I held Mom tightly in my arms, tears fell from my face as I picked up my luggage and headed toward security without a warm goodbye from Dad. I carried the pain of that for a long time.

When I first saw him, he had a faint smile on his face. He looked so much shorter than before, and maybe that was because I had grown up so much since I last saw him. He did not say much, and I could tell from his face he was beyond exhausted after the long hours of his flight.

It must have been a nerve-wracking transit since he did not speak English, just like Mom. I could relate to the challenge of trying to find one's way in a totally strange place.

Though I still had unsettled anger toward Dad, the moment our eyes locked, I decided to be the little girl he used to know. I jumped into his embrace and expressed how much I missed him, like I would have if our family was still together.

He chuckled and held me tightly. When Mom and Kristiaan quickly approached, Dad's smiling face instantly turned into a mixture of confusion and even irritation.

Dad gave me the look of, "Who the heck is this?" He seemed to accuse me of hiding something important from him this whole time.

Kristiaan reached out and shook Dad's hand, and said " 您好, 爸爸! 我的名字是Kristiaan. 很高兴认识您! Nin hao, baba! Wo de mingzi shi Kristiaan. Hen gaoxing renshi nin! (Hello, Dad! My name is Kristiaan. Very happy to meet you.)"

"这是我的男朋友。 (This is my boyfriend,)" I explained to my dad. Kristiaan must have been so nervous that he forgot to share with Dad this important information.

Kristiaan was so scared of how Dad might react. I had spoken nothing of Kristiaan to Dad but had told Kristiaan a lot about my dad. He knew Dad had a terrible temper.

I clenched the hem of my dress as Kristiaan and I waited for Dad's reaction. To both of our surprises, my dad reached out and patted Kristiaan on his back, and said, "也很高兴认识你! (Also, glad to meet you!)"

Before Dad and I realized it, Kristiaan took over my dad's luggage and tried to let Dad walk with me without worrying about anything. Dad seemed to be unimpressed by Kristiaan's gesture and kept walking fast ahead of everyone else, as was typical of him.

When we were in the car, there was an awkward silence again, the same silence that filled the car ride back in Beijing after my parents' divorce. Suddenly, out of nowhere, Dad asked in an assertive tone in Mandarin, "So tell me, Kristiaan, what do you do?"

"我在一个金融公司工作, 是一名首席技术官。Wo zai yige jinrong gongsi gongzuo, shi yiming shouxi jishu guan. (I work at a financial services firm, and I am the CTO.)" He had been brushing up on his Mandarin for the last two months, but it still sounded broken.

"你们交往多久啦? (How long have you guys been dating?)" Dad followed up.

"我们在一起快两年啦。Wo men zai yiqi kuai liangnian la. (We've been together for almost two years,)" Kristiaan replied with careful pronunciations.

Before we picked up Dad, Kristiaan had insisted that he would answer Dad directly, despite my offer to help. He said he wanted to bond with my dad and hopefully earn his approval before my parents left in about ten days.

We arrived at Dad's hotel and helped him settle in his suite about 10:00 p.m. Dad started unpacking his luggage, so we just left him to rest.

When Kristiaan, Mom, and I arrived at Kristiaan's apartment, we gave each other a look of relief. Mom started getting ready for bed.

"Hope that went well." Kristiaan leaned over to me. He finally got to take a deep breath after trying to impress my dad.

***

We woke up at 7:00 a.m. on my Big Day. The lineup of graduates started thirty minutes later. Kristiaan drove Mom, Dad, and I to my drop-off spot, and then he took my parents to their seats on the Quad.

It was a sunny and beautiful day. The families and the graduates had already blocked the streets around the campus, and the students were ready to line up for the ceremony. I stood among my peers, in our graduate gowns and caps. We chatted about the memories we shared as the Class of 2019—singing like no one was watching at Songfest as freshmen or the cut-throat classes we took at the Goizueta Business School.

"This is it!" a girl standing next to me pinched my right arm and chuckled.

And I pinched back. "Hell yeah! We are graduating today!"

Our group started marching toward the designated section on the Quad. Upbeat music was broadcasted on speakers in the background. Professors and Deans lined up on two sides and clapped as the Class of 2019 entered the area right in front of the stage. Every face I saw was filled with pride and joy.

I felt a flood of emotions in my heart. It was bittersweet to march toward the final few hours as a student at Emory. We sat down on the seats reserved for us graduates. Occasionally, my friends spotted me and waved vigorously across several rows.

The ceremony ran the whole morning, with speeches from the president, the class speaker, and many other addresses. The climax finally came when the graduates received their diplomas on stage.

When my name was announced, I proudly walked past the crowd and stepped up to receive my diploma from the Dean.

"Congratulations!" The Dean passed the diploma to me, grabbed my hands with both hands, and shook them excitedly.

When I walked down the stage, Kristiaan was taking photos of me with my parents' phones. Both my mom and dad were cheering for me and clapping. I picked up my speed and rushed into a warm embrace with Kristiaan and my parents. At that moment, we were a family. Regardless of what happened within my family over the past two years, the only thing I cared about was that on my Big Day, everyone was there with me, celebrating my milestone, as one.

It was surreal to think that four years concluded over a four-hour graduation ceremony.

Even more surreal was that my parents and Kristiaan witnessed me receiving the diploma on the stage. The three of them sat together and watched me intently with pride. My parents told me later that Kristiaan translated the ceremony for them the whole time with an app on his phone. And he took advantage of his height to snatch the best photos of me on stage.

It felt impossible to me that my parents could be together for my graduation after the divorce, not to mention their acceptance of Kristiaan's presence. There was still so much to catch up on and so much to be said with this abrupt reunion. Many questions and loose ends still needed to be answered. What would Dad say to me about the divorce? Was he sorry for what he did? How would he react to the fact that his daughter had grown so much and now had a boyfriend?

After the ceremony, Mom, Kristiaan, and I went back to his apartment and collapsed on the bed to take a nap. Dad went to his hotel to rest as well. Whether it was the heat or the intense emotions, we all felt the need to rest.

When we woke up again, it was already 5:00 p.m. Kristiaan had reserved dinner for all of us to celebrate my big day at Sundial, the iconic spinning restaurant on the seventy-second floor of Westin Atlanta, with a sweeping 360-degree view of the city and live jazz.

***

After a wild elevator ride up to the clouds, we were seated at Sundial. We had a window seat that Kristiaan specifically requested for the reservation. The sun started setting and painted the sky with vermillion, baby pink, and a tinge of violet. The colors set the magical tone of the dinner. All of Atlanta was under our view, and the city never looked so gorgeous with its distinctive silhouette carved out by sky-scrapers, the Ferris Wheel, and Mercedes-Benz stadium. Mom and Dad were mesmerized by the sweeping view and seemed to be lost in their own worlds.

"Hi, I'm Chris, your server for the evening. What would you like to drink?" A tall server asked as he came over to our table with a big smile.

"妈妈, 爸爸, 您们想喝什么? Mama, Baba, nin men xiang he shen me? (Mom and Dad, what do you want to drink?)" Kristiaan asked them in broken Mandarin.

Dad seemed to be amused by Kristiaan's pronunciation and his effort. "就点儿水就好。 (Just some water please.)" Dad told me to translate. Mom said the same.

"你为什么爱瑶瑶? (What do you love about Yaoyao?)" Dad asked Kristiaan.

"It's really beyond words, but if I have to verbalize, I would say her intelligence, her unique personality, and her passion in whatever she does. I feel like I won the lottery!" Kristiaan responded in broken Mandarin.

Dad cracked a smile and laughed. Regardless of how intense he might look from the outside, he still had a soft spot for humor. I saw sweat dripping down the side of Kristiaan's face. I knew he was worried that no matter how hard he tried, Dad would not like him.

"Well, I like your humor. However, a relationship is serious business. How do you think you can make her happy?" Dad said in Mandarin and switched his smile back into a poker face again in a blink.

"Umm... I have lots of patience for Yaoyao. I know she has a hot temper sometimes, but I try to make her happy by giving her massages, taking her out to parks, or going hiking. We also know that nothing could not be resolved over bubble tea." Kristiaan switched between Mandarin and the help of a translator app on his phone.

"Anything else? I mean, are you serious about making this long term?" Dad bombarded Kristiaan with more questions in Mandarin.

"Yes. Yaoyao is my world. I want to be with her for life if I have the honor and privilege—"

Kristiaan was interrupted by Dad. "Sure, but I need you to know something. All I hope is that my daughter is happy. I do not wish for her to take on too much stress in life." Dad looked straight into Kristiaan's eyes the whole time he spoke.

Hearing Dad lay out his wishes for me to be happy touched the tender spot in my heart. The two years of silence and hatred for what my dad did to this family were diffused by my realization of his love for me.

"Dad, I promise that making your daughter happy is my number one priority. I will take the stress for both of us to make sure she can pursue whatever her heart desires." Kristiaan meant every word.

Dad went silent. He nodded a few times and seemed a bit more accepting.

"I will see to that. Know that you can never hurt her. She's too trusting to be betrayed."

Dad did not ask another question, while Mom seemed to be stabbed by Dad's words. Tears streamed down Mom's face as she struggled to make sense of what my dad said.

She dabbed her tears with the white napkin on the table. Didn't Dad just shoot himself in the foot? He was definitely not a good example to speak about the importance of never betraying the one you love. I was puzzled yet touched by my dad's words, thinking to myself, "If only he did what he said."

No one really paid any attention to the three-course dinner, but, instead, we were fully engaged in the conversation. I thought a lot about my dad's questions and Kristiaan's responses. Despite his own sins, Dad was trying to be a father again, making sure Kristiaan was the right boyfriend for me. When I thought about Kristiaan's words, I felt lucky he was there to support and love me during my difficult time.

Before we realized it, we were one of the last few tables that still had not left. As the host, Kristiaan got the check despite my parents' insistence on paying the bill.

Before we stood up, Dad told Kristiaan in Mandarin, "I can see how much you love my daughter just by seeing the glow in your eyes when you saw her on the stage at graduation."

Kristiaan was surprised by my dad's approval and could not think of anything other than saying "谢谢! Xie xie! (thank you!)"

The night concluded with a photo of us four with the Atlanta skyline as the background at Sundial. When the camera flashed, I realized I had not taken a new family photo in a long time.

CHAPTER 19

A Glimpse of Home in Atlanta

———

"We should take your parents to do all the things you used to enjoy as a little kid," Kristiaan said when he was designing the itineraries for my parents.

Mom and Dad chose to spend over a week with Kristiaan and I in Atlanta. They missed me much and also wanted to get to know Kristiaan better. One of the activities we planned was taking my parents to the aquarium.

"Aww. You are so sweet. Regardless of what happens between my parents, I want us to at least be family again for over a week." I sighed thinking about how things were different.

Kristiaan went silent and pulled me closer, "I know. But hey, let's look on the bright side. At least we could try to make sure everyone is happy together."

Kristiaan had turned into a dedicated chauffeur and a tour guide. After a short car ride, the four of us arrived at the aquarium's entrance. It was a bright and sunny day with no clouds in sight.

I could not remember the last time I went to the aquarium with Mom and Dad. It must have been so long ago when I was a little girl. I remember Dad enthusiastically pointing out the neon-colored jellyfish and scary-looking sharks. He used to be my guide when we traveled the world, yet now, having explored the other side of the world on my own, I became my dad's guide.

The four of us could not stand side by side among the crowds flooding into the aquarium. Dad and I walked at the front, and Kristiaan and Mom followed. It seemed that regardless of the language barrier, Kristiaan and Mom could casually chat with each other just fine with the help of the language app Kristiaan had downloaded on his phone.

"Mama, I hope you love big sea creatures because what we are going to see today you cannot see anywhere else in the States," I overheard Kristiaan say, getting Mom excited for our time at the aquarium.

"好好! 妈妈很高兴! (Good boy! Mom's very happy!)" Mom was enjoying her chat with Kristiaan.

However, a carefree and lighthearted chat between my dad and I was not at all intuitive. The contrast between the front row and the back was ironic. Kristiaan and Mom just met a few days ago, and they were already chatting like family. However, although Dad and I had known each other since I was born, starting a joyful conversation with him was challenging. His divorce from Mom pushed us further apart, and there seemed to be an unspeakable wall between us that was too heavy to even open up the conversation.

Dad and I walked together quietly. He left me no choice but to break the silence by pointing at sea lions, belugas, or otters around to cheer him up.

"老爸, 快看! 白鲸在水里吐泡泡儿哪! (Look, Dad! The Belugas are blowing bubbles in the water!)" I was excited to see a couple of Belugas blowing bubbles in heart shapes. Dad seemed to be amused by the heart-shaped bubbles, so he stopped and watched it with me.

My excitement felt familiar, as if I switched roles with Dad when we went to the aquarium when I was a little girl. I showed him the amazing creatures around us to inspire his curious mind. Dad did not say anything, but his eyes went wider and he grinned. His smile was filled with joy, which I had not seen with my own eyes for a long time. Not connecting with him for two years made me feel distant from him, not to mention the fact that it was common for him to have a poker face.

Kristiaan switched places with me so he could walk with Dad for a while. Kristiaan led us toward the iconic whale sharks section. I held Mom's hands and watched Kristiaan try to bond with my dad at the front. Their chats were too vague for me to catch, but from the look of Dad's cheerful facial expression, I could tell Kristiaan entertained him with his humor again.

After walking through a dark passage, we stopped in front of an aquarium that looked like a movie screen where whale sharks swam casually with countless other marine animals such as small sharks, manta rays, and sea turtles. Standing in front of a shark tank the size of a football field made us feel so small.

"哇！这太壮观了！ (This is incredible!)" Dad froze in front of the whale sharks, which are the largest fish in the world. He seemed elated.

Mom also showed her bewilderment. My parents' pure happiness reminded me of what it was like for us three to enjoy the aquarium together when I was little.

"看！这有一条, 两条… (Look! There's one, two...)" Mom started counting how many whale sharks there were.

"一共五条！ (There are five in total!)" Dad hollered confidently.

At that moment, though I was astonished by the magnificent whale sharks, my eyes were fixated on my parents. Looking at their cheerful faces again made me feel like we were a complete family again. The sense of belonging was so intense it almost made me believe the divorce did not happen. We loved our time at the aquarium together like we used to, nothing different.

We stood in front of the big-screen-like exhibit for a long time and lost track of time. I wanted it to last forever so I could indulge in my stolen "family time." While counting whale sharks, my parents and I savored our time together like we used to. Even if it was just a couple of sweet hours at the aquarium, we left with a memory I could keep dreaming of at night.

***

Spring blossoms ferociously during the ides of May. Looking around, one might find themselves bedazzled by a burst of colors. Sweet violet lilacs, peonies in fuchsia, cream, or wine, and bountiful ivory magnolias with a hint of pearl pink sprinkle magic in the air.

Though Kristiaan would have loved to show my parents Atlanta every day when they were in town, he could not get every day off from work. On a warm and cozy Wednesday, I told Kristiaan to catch up on his work projects and decided to take my parents to the zoo.

It would be the first day since they arrived that the three of us spent a day without Kristiaan. I had been hoping that Kristiaan's presence would reduce the possibility of any conflicts between Mom and Dad, or between my dad and I. At least, as Dad used to say, "Keep family issues within the family." It was hard for me to fathom, with so many grievances among the three of us, coupled with the long period of silence and separation, what frictions would occur when we were alone together.

We arrived at Zoo Atlanta a few minutes later after a short ride.

I tried to stand in the middle between my parents so Mom would not feel awkward having to walk with my dad. I held Mom's hand with my right hand and Dad's with my left. As I walked side-by-side with them, flashbacks of my childhood came back to me again. The times when we went to feed giraffes or watch dolphin shows at the aquarium emerged in my head like a movie. We used to sit by the alligator section and count how many sunbathing alligators had their mouths wide open. Dad always bought me a jumbo unicorn cotton candy at the end of our visit. He knew some sweetness would put a smile on my face.

Though I knew those memories would never happen again, I still hoped we could feel like family again, even if it was only for a day.

"在一起的感觉真好。 (It feels good to be together again,)" I said to them. The moment those words came out of my mouth, I realized I made a mistake. Mom would probably feel upset, and Dad—who knew what he would think. But to my surprise, they both chuckled with joy. It gave me hope that we could relive some of those joyous zoo memories.

"看! 这个白孔雀要开屏了! (Look! The white peacock is about to show off its feathers!)" I squeaked.

My parents froze as well, and the three of us intently watched the mystic creature flex its feathers like a majestic wedding gown.

"真美呀。 (So beautiful.)" Mom's eyes were glued to the ivory princess. Dad went speechless and was completely in awe. The stunning beauty connected the three of us as we shared the magical moment together.

"感激当下呀。 (Be grateful for the present.)" Dad expressed his gratitude. He read my mind, and I believed my mom felt it too.

I wondered to myself what happiness was after all. When I saw the sparkles in my mom and dad's eyes as we enjoyed the magnificent show from the white peacock, I thought that was happiness to me. I believed my parents knew that all I hoped for, especially during my graduation week, was for us to be together.

We spent a very lovely and carefree time at the zoo. We were thrilled to see many adorable animals—flamingos, elephants, gorillas—just like we used to love. There were no conflicts, no drama, and nothing to remind me of the pain in the past. Whether we were a family again or not no longer puzzled me. All that mattered was that we were blissful again, for as long as we wanted it to be.

***

My parents' visit to Atlanta was a great excuse for Kristiaan and I to be tourists in the city we had lived in for years. One of the items on the bucket list for first-timers in Atlanta was watching the sunset from Skyview Atlanta, a twenty-story Ferris wheel at Centennial Park.

Two days later on a Thursday evening, when the sun started to paint the sky in pearl pink, hot red, and magenta, Kristiaan took my family to ride the Ferris wheel. It was a busy evening, and the traffic around Centennial Park was especially stagnant.

"Once I find a spot to pull over on the other side of the park, you just hop off and take your parents to the wheel first, okay? I will catch you guys soon after." Kristiaan wanted to save as much time as we could so we could hop onto the Ferris wheel to enjoy the sunset before it vanished.

Kristiaan found a spot a block away from where we were supposed to be. I quickly hopped out and dragged my parents toward the wheel.

Mom and Dad looked confused, and I explained while sprinting, "快到时间了。(It's almost time.)"

"看谁跑得快！(See who runs the fastest!)" Dad took bigger strides and waved his arms back and forth like a professional athlete.

Mom did not want to be left behind. She pointed her head forward and ran like a bullet. By the time we crossed Centennial Park, we were out of breath, and we burst into laughter.

"体力可不如以前了！ (My stamina is not like before!)" Dad lamented.

I pointed up to the sky, and my parents saw the big Ferris wheel standing tall across the street. The wheel looked particularly radiant when the sky started turning dark. Streams of neon lights curved out the silhouette of the wheel with glowing colors of the rainbow.

When we approached the entrance, I was disappointed by the serpentine line. While standing in line, my heart started beating fast as I became more anxious. I turned my head around and looked across the park, but Kristiaan was still nowhere in sight.

We had run so hard just to make sure we made it on time. What if we miss the sunset?

"Here I am! We are gonna make it." Kristiaan said as he ran up to us, panting hard.

About ten minutes later, the staff started letting more people onto the carts. We were the last ones before the staff cut off the line and closed the gate. Dad insisted Kristiaan and I sit together as we started to rise to the sky slowly. My parents sat together across from me. Mom pulled out her phone and started taking photos of Kristiaan and I with the blazing sunset and Atlanta's skyline in the background. When the warm vermilion sunrays projected onto my parents' happy faces, they looked so beautiful together. Their smiles glowed with the sunset. It was a movie-like dream, a picture that would be forever imprinted in my head.

Before we realized it, we were at the top of the wheel. The four of us were mesmerized by the burning sunset stretching into the horizon and the silhouette of midtown Atlanta, which looked like a dragon's backbone.

When my parents gazed into the distance, I quickly snapped a few photos of the calm on their faces. I looked at the photos I took on my phone and then looked at my parents. The photos could not vividly capture the happiness blooming on their faces. I tried my best to capture this moment. Nothing could make me happier than the four of us being together.

***

How should I spend the last few hours with my parents before they fly back? I wondered. Today was the day before their flights back home.

Mom had to pack because she would leave early in the morning. Though Mom could not join us, Kristiaan took Dad and I to have some oysters at The Optimist during its famous happy hour in the afternoon on Saturdays. The Optimist is a chic restaurant tucked in the busy, downtown food haven of Atlanta. It had a tiny mini-golf course in its backyard. When we arrived, Kristiaan picked a table right by the window with abundant sunshine.

We ordered three dozen oysters of over six kinds, some from the West coast, others from the East. Dad always picked the biggest and deepest oyster shells and put them on my plate.

"老爸！您应该多吃点儿。 (Dad! You should eat more.)" I would shovel those oysters back on Dad's plate.

"好吃吗? Hao chi ma? (Do they taste good?)" Kristiaan tried to ask Dad in Mandarin.

"好吃! 很清爽。 (Very tasty! Refreshing.)" Dad took a slurp of a deep-cup oyster and chewed it with much satisfaction.

I loved watching Dad enjoy his oysters. I took another meaty oyster, dripped some Sriracha and seafood sauce on top, and placed it on Dad's plate.

Dad started chatting with me about what happened during the past two years. I shared with him that I tried to keep up with schoolwork and navigate my career path in branding, or any roles in the creative industries. Then I briefed him on how I met Kristiaan and how he had been super supportive in my life. The only thing I avoided sharing was how depressed I was after his divorce from Mom. It was too traumatic to even begin to rewind. I had been trying for months not to think about it and get as far from the trauma as possible. Just as I was trying to give an optimistic presentation of my life over the past two years, Dad suddenly said something that hit me like a brick.

"瑶瑶, 老爸对不起你。 (Yaoyao, I want to tell you that I am sorry.)" Dad interrupted my orchestrated and sugar-coated speech and looked me in the eyes across the table.

At first, I could not believe what I heard. Of all the people in my life, the last person I expected an apology from was my dad. He was always so right, so domineering that even the slightest doubt on his authority induced an explosive tirade from him. Even if he was wrong, he would blame me.

I also could not believe that the apology I had wanted for years could happen just like that.

I was frozen, eyes wide open, staring at Dad without knowing what to say. My first feeling was anger. All this time, he had a chance to confess to me what he did wrong, but he chose to stay silent and could not get over his ego. Next, I felt bitterness. How could Dad know all the dark nights when I cried myself to sleep and the countless days when I was in pain? When I was feeling lost, sad, and torn apart, where was he? What was he thinking when he cut this family in half?

The next thing Dad said pushed me further into emotional turmoil.

"我知道你一个人不容易。爸爸对不起你。 (I understand that going through all this on your own is not easy. Dad is sorry.)" He reached out his hands and tried to hold mine across the table. His voice was shaking as he spoke.

I tried to avoid eye contact with him because I could not bear to show my dad how much he hurt me. But I couldn't hide it; tears streamed down my face, and I started sobbing. Over two years of crying myself to sleep at night, over two years of wandering around the world alone, and over two years of trying to find home were all condensed in my tears. I could not possibly put this long period of bereavement into words and explain it to Dad.

As much as I tried to reject his apology, I could not deny the days and nights when I wished I could get an explanation or any trace of empathy from him. All I wanted was an answer that could pull me out of my misery of meandering without roots, out of the nightmare of having a broken home, and out of the trauma of losing a once happy and complete family.

I clenched my dad's hands and held them tightly. Words still could not come out of my mouth, so I just nodded incessantly. By reacting to Dad's words, I accepted his flaws, the pain he caused this family, but I also simultaneously accepted his long-overdue apology.

An idiom in Mandarin goes like this: "解铃还需系铃人。 Only the person who tied a bell on the tiger's neck can untie the bell." It implies a problem can only be solved by whoever caused it.

When Dad apologized to me, he at least attempted to untie the knot he built between us—the unspoken tension that existed for years. I still needed to figure out how my relationship with my dad would develop from that point on. How should I reconnect with him now that he had apologized? How could I trust him again when I felt betrayed this whole time? What would forgiveness mean? At the very least, the defining moment when he apologized was an optimistic start.

Kristiaan silently witnessed the heartfelt moment throughout. It seemed like he could understand what was happening regardless of the language barrier. He tried to let my dad and I have the moment for ourselves.

CHAPTER 20

Rooted in Beijing

———

"Ladies and Gentlemen. We've landed at Beijing Capital International Airport. Thanks so much for flying with Air China. We hope that you enjoyed a wonderful flight," a flight attendant announced.

I rubbed my drowsy eyes and stretched my sore back and arms after the excruciatingly long flight. Outside the window, the early evening sunshine was bright and welcoming.

No matter where I traveled in the world, my hometown summoned me back. Beijing was the place where I grew up and made my memories as a child and adolescent. Many nights when I dreamed on the other side of the world, I found myself in my hometown strolling among majestic palaces with rouge walls and gold roofs. In my dreams, I savored the sinfully delicious 北京烤鸭 *Peking Duck*—golden crispy crust with soft meat inside. Best of all, I sat at Grandma's kitchen table again, savoring the taste of home with her most favorite home-cooked meals. These dreams were a wonderful escape.

No matter how many years I had been away, the moment I landed, I instantly felt like a child rushing into my mom's arms. Throughout my college years, I had only gone back to Beijing three times. Every time I returned, I found myself struggling to keep up with all the changes. The pet store where my mom and I used to get my bunnies or goldfish was torn down; a skyscraper replaced it instead. The massive shopping mall where my family used to get decor for the Spring Festival was renovated and expanded so much that it was unrecognizable from the outside. I wondered what would be new this time.

The moment I arrived at the pickup area, I noticed right away that Mom had gotten a new hairstyle. Her hair curled into loose waves like a bouquet of roses blooming on her head. Mom's skin was luminescent as usual. Her smile was glowing and reflected a hint of pearl pink on her cheeks. Her lips were glazed with cherry red lip gloss that seemed almost edible. Mom must have been in good spirits and polished her look to every last detail.

"Ma!" I rushed to hug her.

Mom held me tightly in her arms and whispered, "好想你啊! (Missed you so much!)"

Then, Mom told me not to tell Dad I was back. I was confused and wanted to ask her why. When the words were just about to come out of my mouth, I realized the reason was obvious. Mom wanted my time home to be relaxing and not to be split between two places constantly. I also could not wait to spend more time with Grandma, my mom's mom. Mom and I would stay at Grandma's house. I could see it would be girls' bonding time. *That's probably why Mom looks radiant, she is finally free from my dad.* I thought.

Mom drove me to Grandma's place. On the way, I stared out of the window and observed the overwhelming changes.

I tried to process the scene in front of my eyes. 胡同 *Hu Tong* (narrow alleys) were expanded into four-lane roads where cars sped by. Some 四合院 *Si He Yuan* (traditional courtyard residences) were renovated into modern hotels that lacked any respect for tradition. Part of me felt despair that Beijing had lost part of its cultural heritage that defined its identity.

Mom said new rules were imposed not long ago. No more fireworks were allowed in the metro area during the Chinese New Year for safety reasons. The Spring Festival was much quieter these days, not loud and boisterous like before.

The home I used to know has changed so much it even makes me feel foreign. My thoughts raced as I connected my observations with the information from Mom. I realized right then that the home I lost was not just the complete family I used to have but also the city I used to live in. I was so afraid that one day when I flew back again, I would be a total stranger in the city where I was born.

***

Mom parked her car next to my grandma's place. Grandma's house still looked the same just like years ago when I was a little kid listening to her bedtime stories on mid-summer nights and going to the fish market with her. Grandma loved growing herbs, shrubs, and sometimes even strawberries and aloe. She could get her ingredients for dinner straight from her garden. "纯天然。没化学物质。 (It's organic! No chemicals.)" Grandma would show off her freshly grown fruits or veggies.

Mom and I stepped into Grandma's house. Grandma ran toward the door, and to my surprise, she seemed so short and small. It was definitely not the strong and tall Grandma I knew as a kid. There's a saying in Mandarin: "时间是把杀猪的刀。 (Time is like a knife used to kill a pig, slow yet cruel.)" Tears welled up in my eyes as I was reminded of how time flies.

"瑶瑶! 都这么高啦。 (You've grown so tall!)" Grandma hollered.

I scooped her up into my arms. Somehow my grandma was lifted off the ground without me even trying as I hugged her. The days when Grandma took me to parks and cooked me yummy meals flashed in front of my eyes. I felt guilty that I had not spent more time with her. *I must have been a terrible granddaughter,* I thought.

The dusk had arrived, and the night fell like a dark blue curtain.

"你饿了吧! 想吃点儿什么？ (Bet you are hungry! What do you want to eat for dinner?)" Grandma was motivated to fill my tummy as usual.

Mom interrupted and said she would cook instead so that Grandma and I could relax and enjoy our long-overdue chat. Mom ended up making porridge, sweet and chewy.

Grandma could not stop studying me from head to toe. She was amazed by how much I had grown up. "大学毕业生啦! (You are a college graduate now!)" Grandma patted my back, her eyes full of pride.

"姥姥, 咱们玩儿盘五子儿棋吧! (Grandma, let's play Gomoku!)" I pulled out the chessboard beneath Grandma's dresser.

Grandma and I loved playing 五子棋 *Wu Zi Qi*, Gomoku, also called Five in a Row. I recalled spending lazy evenings playing Gomoku with Grandma. Whoever won the game grabbed a handful of candies from the China jar in the kitchen. By the end of the game, Grandma accused me of eating too many sweets, and she warned me, "吃糖太多 容易有蛀牙！(Eating too many candies causes cavities!)"

We started playing Gomoku again, and I instantly felt like I traveled back in time. I knew playing Gomoku would put a smile on Grandma's face. Over the past four years, she must have missed spending time with me. I wondered how many times Grandma wanted to play Gomoku but could not find me around her house. While tossing my black stones on the board, I thought, *I need to come home more often and spend time with Grandma.*

I found Grandma's pensive look adorable and knew all she ever wanted was to have me by her side. She seemed so content and delighted when we revisited our little tradition. I did not need to travel to find what I needed the most because family was right there with me.

When I was with Grandma, I felt rooted at home again. It seemed that no matter where I was in the world, my grandma was always there hoping I'd return to her. To me, she was the person who safeguarded my memories in Beijing, and those countless happy childhood days that never seemed to end. It dawned on me that no matter how much the city had changed, as long as I came back to Grandma, Beijing would always be the same as I knew as a kid.

"饭来咯！(Dinner is served!)" Mom came out of the kitchen with three bowls of steamy porridge.

Mom, Grandma, and I enjoyed our dinner together. Finally, after years, I got a taste of Mom's cooking again. The taste of home that seemed so distant when I was away melted in my mouth and warmed up my body. The exhaustion from traveling and the long nights of homesickness vanished into thin air.

CHAPTER 21

Summer With Grandma

—

At Grandma's house, my childhood came back to me as if I was that chipper three-year-old running around her garden again. The most simple and even boring things I used to do with 姥姥 Laolao (my grandma's nickname) held a special place in my heart now. I dreamed of them many nights when I was away. Upon my return to Beijing, I tried to do them with my grandma all over again.

In the morning, Laolao and I would go to the famous 牛街 *Niu Jie* (Bull Street) and savor all kinds of traditional breakfast dishes indigenous to Beijingers, such as 豆腐脑 *Dou Fu Nao* (veggie tofu stew), 糖油饼 *Tang You Bing* (sugar-diced fried dough), and 豆浆 *Dou Jiang* (soy milk). When I was little, my grandma and I went to *Niu Jie* all the time; it was food heaven for us.

We stuffed our tummies with yummy food to our hearts' content, we would venture into the parks where we used to spend many long afternoons.

One of the parks Laolao and I revisited during the month I spent in Beijing was 颐和园 *The Summer Palace*. It is an imperial garden where the emperors in the Qing Dynasty relaxed and sought coolness amid the hottest days in summer. Beijingers are privileged to be able to enjoy such a treat in a paradise of lakes, gardens, and palaces that used to accommodate emperors.

昆明湖 *Kunming Lake* sits at the heart of the gardens where my grandma and I loved boating. Looking around, we could see willow trees flowing in the summer breeze like girls letting their long hair loose by the lake. Many temples and palaces were tucked in the greens and showed off the top of their golden roofs shining in the sun.

When Grandma and I hopped on a boat, we usually brought some snacks with us, and sometimes a card game or chess to kill our time on the lake. 艾窝窝 *Ai Wo Wo*, a traditional Beijing snack made of a sticky rice bun stuffed with red bean sauce, was our top choice. The red beans and the honey-glazed rice melted in our mouths. As a little girl, I often imagined that happiness tasted just like *Ai Wo Wo*—sweet, sticky, and chewy.

"Laolao, to be honest, I don't know how I survived these past few years after my parents' divorce," I said in Mandarin, sighing.

"I understand, sweetheart. You have all reason to be confused. Grandma knows." Grandma peddled the boat softly.

A few ripples formed as the breeze glazed across the surface of the lake. The sunbeams danced on the ripples like millions of diamonds on silky fabric. I bet the fine fabrics the royalties in the Qing dynasty used to wear looked just like that.

"As you gather more experiences in life, the worries you have right now might not seem so gripping anymore. Trust me, things will get better if you choose," Grandma said as we hopped off our boat.

When I walked back toward Grandma's house holding her hand, I recalled what she used to say whenever I struggled with challenges within my family. "家家有本儿难念的经。(Every family has gone through difficulties unknown by the public.)" Grandma liked to console me when my parents quarreled, and encouraged me to see family issues as a common part of life.

The moment I thought of her reminder, she spoke of it again. Her words offered me some strength to believe I would find a way to break free from the struggles I had with my parents' divorce.

***

In the evenings, Laolao cooked my favorite dishes again. During the month we were together, Grandma pampered me with her signature beef broth and hot pot. Her dishes reminded me of the taste of home I had missed so much when I was away.

When Grandma and I were about to go to bed, I deliberately snuggled up to her in bed and demanded she tell me the bedtime stories I fell asleep with when I was a child.

"You are lucky, you know that? When I was young, China was not yet developed like today. Our generation did not grow up with ample education resources, fancy clothes and cars, or skyscrapers."

I instantly felt my whole body relax and focus on listening to her soothing voice.

"Back in the days, I took on so many different challenging works as a young girl. And I don't think you could even imagine—assembling pieces at factories, sewing, coordinating at hospitals, when I was barely eighteen. But look how happy I am now with my best granddaughter. I think those experiences only make me stronger. I think the same goes for you."

"I see, Laolao," I replied as Grandma's words sunk into my head.

"Good girl. You are smart to understand this. In terms of your parents' divorce, you should live your own life and try to build your own happiness. What happens between them should not be the reason why you are miserable." Grandma held me in her arms as we lay down side by side.

"Laolao, do you miss Grandpa?" I asked.

"Of course."

Grandma married twice. My biological grandpa died of cancer when my mom was only sixteen. Then my grandma remarried. However, my step grandpa died a few years back as well. She had been alone on her own ever since and rarely spoke about my biological grandpa. I never met my real grandpa, but my step grandpa loved me dearly. When he was alive, my grandma quarreled with him on a daily basis, and most of the time, out of love.

I remembered that my step grandpa had high blood sugar. Grandma used to make a large bowl of salad of fruits and nuts, which were helpful for Grandpa to lower his blood sugar. Fresh fruits and nuts were not Grandpa's favorite, so he vehemently refused whenever Grandma placed the salad by his bed in the morning. "Why are you so stubborn?" Grandma would yell at him with frustration. Grandpa either gave my grandma the silent treatment or yelled back and said, "I hate fruits and nuts!" It was not easy for my grandma to step down, so she often said, "If you don't finish the salad, then no TV for you today!"

Grandpa could not live without his favorite TV shows, so he usually conceded to my grandma and finished the whole salad bowl without any more complaints.

"Marriages are not always perfect. When you grow older, you will be able to understand that companionship is more important than perfection," Grandma said.

With Grandma's bedtime story easing my worries, the singing cicadas, and the clapping leaves in the breeze, I slowly closed my eyes. Soon I was lost in my sweet dreamland, where I had yearned to return. During the time I spent at home with Laolao, I could savor the cloying wonderlands in my dreams again. Like a bear fainted in its honey jar, I slept soundly and probably snored and drooled, with Grandma's stories replaying in my dreams.

***

I dug through some boxes covered with thick layers of dust under her bed. Grandma's room was a mini museum of our family history. Searching through the physical documentation of my family's past was like a treasure hunt. As I flipped through the wooden boxes of different sizes, my heart started pounding faster, thrilled yet nervous.

Among the scattered items stacked in the boxes, I unearthed Grandma's old diploma with dark yellow tainting the corners, Grandma's wedding photo album, and her favorite books. I was impressed by the glowing young lady in the photos taken in her late twenties. Grandma wore hot red lipstick and had such a glamorous smile. Her long dark hair naturally landed on her shoulders. Her eyes were shining and brought the dull and wrinkled photos to life.

I wondered what was going through her mind when she was my age. *Did Grandma also wonder about what home means? Did Grandma also ponder what makes a happy and healthy relationship?*

As I lost myself in the thoughts of my grandma's younger days, I heard the door crack open.

"Yaoyao, what are you doing sitting on the floor?" Grandma asked as she stepped into her bedroom after returning from the fish market.

"I just... I was curious...I mean...," I stammered as my thoughts tangled up like a bundle of ropes.

Would Grandma be mad that I opened all of her boxes behind her back? I felt cold sweat drip down along my spine, making my T-shirt wet and sticky.

"I see that you've found quite some treasures!" Grandma stepped over and sat on her bed. "Surprised? Grandma was just like you once."

I stood up from the floor and sat next to Grandma. "Could you tell me the stories of these photos?"

"I used to love makeup. So you can see, in most of the photos, I looked like a posh cover girl. And these photos were taken before my wedding. I was wearing my mom's gown." Grandma was pointing at a few photos and looked elated.

"Are there other albums that you want to show me?" I asked.

"Sure, there are so many old albums. Here, let me see what I can find."

Grandma diligently flipped through her boxes and carefully singled out the photo albums. Among the ones she found, two stood out to me from the rest. One contained my parents' wedding photos, and another included my fine art photos taken when I was seven.

I took the heavy albums from Grandma and started perusing each photo. The weight of frozen memories pressed my hands down onto my lap. Grandma left the room and let me have my own space.

In the wedding photos, Mom wore a dreamy ivory gown embroidered with romantic lace and exquisite feathery floral embellishments. Mom's hair was nicely braided and pinned with fresh pearl pink roses. She had a matching rosy smile with blushed cheeks.

In one photo, her eyes were closed, making her look like she was immersed in a sweet dream. Her head leaned slightly onto her right shoulder, where a large bouquet of fuchsia pink roses rested. Standing right behind her was Dad, his arms wrapped tightly around her.

Dad had his eyes closed in that photo as well, and his head leaned on Mom's. His arms enclosed Mom's arms and held the roses on her right shoulder. Dad wore a dark maroon tuxedo, dandy and sleek.

These snapshots of love almost made me feel like I was there with Mom and Dad for the most sacred ceremony of their lives. Their obvious happiness made me wonder what brought them together in such a way that they promised to spend the rest of their lives together. I wondered if I would feel just as happy, if not more, as my parents on my future wedding day. If Kristiaan and I ended up together, would our relationship crumble like my parents'?

When I flipped through the rest of the album, I suddenly woke up from the sweet dream and realized these fairytales of parents only made the current reality of my family even more cutting. The old wedding photo album became a heavy satire to the promise of a lasting and happy marriage.

All a bunch of bullshit, I thought to myself and punched the cover of the album.

Then I picked up the other photo album. There was an intense glow in my eyes when I was seven. I seemed to have the capacity to trust the good in people. However, after my parents' divorce, I lost that leap of faith because my dad's betrayal shifted my worldview. Looking at the photos of me and looking at myself in the mirror in my grandma's bedroom, I could not reconcile the two images of me. Tears well up in my eyes and blurred the view of everything around me until it looked like a watercolor painting.

Grandma entered the room again.

"Why don't we put these albums back where they were? There's a reason why Grandma put them in boxes under the bed." Grandma tucked the albums in the bottom of the wooden box and shoved it under the bed.

I reached out and held my grandma tightly.

"You need to cheer up and stop crying so much. Come! Let's make some eggs. Nothing cannot be resolved over a good breakfast for dinner!" Grandma said.

The thought of returning to the little tradition that Grandma and I had put a grin on my face. We headed to the kitchen, leaving those old albums quietly sealed in the boxes under her bed.

CHAPTER 22

Mom's Love Story

———

On a Sunday afternoon, with a mild breeze flowing through our hair, Mom and I walked our two dogs, Honey—an Alaskan malamute—and Dots—a hybrid, along the river not far from where Mom lived. Not a cloud was in sight. The weather was perfect for kite flying. Some locals brought their kites of all shapes, and a colorful octopus, swallow, and butterfly soared among the birds in the sapphire sky.

Still thinking about the old photo albums I saw at Grandma's, with photographs of my mother and father embracing tenderly as I'd never seen them do, I said, "Mom, I have been wondering what your past relationships looked like." I said this out of the blue in Mandarin, linking arms with her. I continued, "I don't think we ever talked about them in detail before."

"My relationships? Why?" Mom was startled by my question.

"Just curious."

"Ok... Where do you want me to start?"

"Why don't you tell me about your first boyfriend?"

"I was eighteen. Our families lived very close to each other. And during our free time, we would hang out. But when they moved, we had to break up after an almost two-year relationship." Mom spoke about her first love without any emotion.

I was expecting her to tell me about a heartbreaking first romance of two star-crossed lovers who had to murder their love as life took them separate ways. However, Mom was indifferent.

How could Mom be so aloof about her first love? Wouldn't she at least feel sad that it didn't work out? Questions piled up in my head, and I wondered how my mom could be so cold.

"What happened after? I mean your other boyfriends?"

"There were a couple of boys I had been with before your dad. I met them during college. We had a lot of fun together. However, the relationships all ended at last because..." Mom suddenly paused, and she seemed to lose herself in her own thoughts.

"Mom, you okay?" I asked, waking her from her world.

"I'm fine. What was I saying?" Mom seemed absent-minded.

"You said those relationships ended, but you have yet to offer a reason," I said, demanding that Mom finish her stories.

"They were all amazing, but I just don't think those boys were mature enough. One of them kept switching jobs, and it was hard to see our future. Remember, it was not long after I lost your grandpa. At that point, I needed stability above anything." Mom's voice was crisp and assertive.

My mom's dad passed away when Mom was just about to head to college. He was an up-and-coming entrepreneur who owned multiple factories producing glass ampoule cutters. Grandpa died of lung cancer in his late forties. Mom always said Grandpa was the person she aspired to become—creative, responsible, and brave. Grandpa was the person I always wished to meet but couldn't.

Mom shared how she was devastated when her dad died when she was still a teenager. She said a swarm of fears for the future and insecurities crept into her psyche. I could understand why stability and accountability were so important to Mom when she was dating.

An immediate thought flashed across my mind. *Does Mom regret meeting Dad? How did she cope with the trauma of divorce?*

"Mom?" I pulled Mom back from her roaming thoughts.

"Yes?" Mom looked back at me. Sunshine shimmered on her face and made her skin looked luminescent.

"Do you have regrets about Dad? Like, do you wish you had never committed to him?" I regretted the moment I asked those questions. Though my intense curiosity pushed me to ask more, I did not want Mom to relive her traumatic experience with my dad. I wished she could choose someone else who could make her happy, if only she could travel back in time.

"I don't. Even if I do, what does it matter now?"

"Do you not wish you had a partner to grow old with you?" I was utterly confused.

"I loved your Dad. Before we had you, we were madly in love. He used to not be like this. People change, you know? I couldn't possibly tell back then. After you were born, I started noticing his demons—his playboy spirit resurfaced and his increasingly explosive temper," Mom explained. "There's no use talking about these now. I don't regret a thing because had I not been with him, I would not have you! You are the best thing that could happen in my life."

"I love you, Mom!" I pulled my mom into a heartfelt embrace and tears of joy welled up in my eyes.

"I love you the most," Mom whispered.

We continued strolling along the river. I could not help but replay Mom's love stories in my head and wondered if she had found someone new to make her happy again.

***

"Meet my boyfriend, Song." In Mandarin, Mom introduced me to her new love at his three-bedroom apartment, two days later.

What? This cannot be true! I gasped and could not believe the weird plan the universe had for us.

Song is the father of my childhood friend, Chan, who went to the same primary school with me, took English lessons with me, and grew up with me until I left for college in the states.

Chan lost her mom, Ying, in early 2016, which was a tough year not only for Chan's family but also for my mom, who used to be Ying's best friend. While Chan and I took dance classes and swam in the pool, our moms used to go shopping or chat about anything from parenting to their own secrets. Ying died of cancer, which was diagnosed as terminal when she was sent to the hospital. She did not live more than six months after the diagnosis. When Ying went through chemotherapy with excruciating pain and hair loss, Mom spent hours and days attending to her needs.

One day, Ying never woke up again. It was an earth-shattering event in Chan's life. Because my mom and Chan's mom were confidants, my mom was close to Chan as well. Our parents used to joke a lot about switching daughters because our families got along seamlessly well. I didn't know what happened after Ying's passing.

I thought about Chan's father. I remembered his mild and amicable personality, a stark contrast to my dad's explosive temper. Song beamed like a child every time he saw me. He used to tutor me in math when I was in primary school and middle school because he was a tech nerd. We had not seen each other for years since Chan and I pursued different colleges and career paths.

"瑶瑶，又见面啦！都这么高了。(Yaoyao, good to see you again! You've grown so tall.)" Song was amazed when he saw me. I bet he could not believe how much I had evolved from the artless and naive little girl he knew. Indeed, I could barely reach his shoulders when I was younger, and now I was at eye level. He did not change much other than a hint of grey hair on his head.

While Song began preparing dinner for Mom and I, she said they had been together for a while and waited until I came back to break the news. I did not know Mom had been dating for about a year. It was a wonderful surprise. Just from the way Song and Mom gazed at each other, I knew they loved each other immensely.

"He told me that he had been secretly liking me, and he could not believe that the time finally came for him to confess." Mom smirked while she shared the story with me.

"I'm so happy for you, Mom. Are you happy with him?"

"He's nothing like your dad. In fact, quite the opposite; he's caring, patient, and funny, whereas your dad... you know your dad."

I could tell from the way Mom described him that she had fallen in love with Song. It was hard for me to wrap my head around the dramatic change in my mom's love life. *How should I react in front of Song now? He is not my dad, but he is sort of playing my dad's role now.*

"He cooks for me every day and gives me full-body massages. He's not smart with words, but he is a doer," Mom continued.

"Wow, sounds like an experience that I can relate to!" I chuckled at the uncanny similarity between my mom's relationship with Song and mine with Kristiaan.

Both Kristiaan and Song are tech nerds. They are patient, well-tempered, and loving. Song might have a competitive advantage; he is a talented cook.

"I knew our fates were synced in some way." Mom pinched my right arm playfully. "I am so glad that you have Kristiaan by your side while you are healing."

Song walked out of the kitchen with grilled asparagus, duck stew, pancakes, and boiled sweet corn. It was a feast! The dishes were not only appealing in colors but also mesmerizing in aroma.

I could not wait any longer, so I picked up my chopsticks and put some food into my mouth. *This is ridiculously delicious!* I thought. For years, my dad cooked no more than once for Mom and I. Song's cooking gave me a sense of what it would feel like to taste home dishes prepared by a dad. The food soothed my conflicting thoughts and helped me clear my mind. *No wonder Mom fell in love with him!*

Knowing that Song had been taking care of Mom since her divorce assured me she was in good hands. She deserved the world, and I was so pleased she found a partner who matched her trust and affection.

"好吃吗? (Tastes good?)" Song asked me.

"倍儿香! (Yummy!)" I savored the dinner so much I did not even look at him when I replied.

We had our dinner at one big table, forming a new home beyond my expectations. At first, my instinct told me to reject Song because, after all, he was not my dad. I even thought about giving him a hard time. However, since he made my mom happy and helped her power through her most difficult time in life, I knew I should give them my blessing. *Even though the new home I have is not perfect,* I thought, *it is enough for Mom to lean on the person she loves and live without fear and sadness.*

After dinner, Song suggested we play cards. The three of us sat at the corners of a king-sized bed and played cards all night long. Part of me felt content that Mom and Song loved each other and that we became a new unit, but another part of me felt melancholy.

The person who used to sit at Song's spot was my dad. If only I could travel back in time and play board games with my mom and my dad together as a family.

That night when I went to sleep next to Mom, I stared at the ceiling and my mind drifted away.

"Mom, how could you love again after being deeply betrayed and hurt?" I asked her quietly.

"Sometimes you have to surrender to the universe. Song has been around in my life, and now he has become even more important to me. I did not give up on my chance to be happy again. I know it feels scary, especially given the betrayal I suffered from your dad. However, you cannot let one person destroy your capacity to love, no?" Mom turned toward me and wrapped her arms around my shoulders.

"Mmm, I hope I never need to go through it. However, if I do, I will remember what you said." I closed my eyes with Mom's words and her love stories in mind, and gradually lost myself in dreamland.

CHAPTER 23

An Empty Palace

———

Dad's art gallery is located inside an ancient palace that used to belong to an emperor. The palace was a sacred place where the emperor prayed for gods and goddesses to summon abundant rain to grow the crops that could bring wealth and prosperity to his people. Dad thought it might bring good luck to his art gallery business.

The art gallery had been open for almost a decade. The palace did bring some fortune to my dad's business. With Dad's well-connected network thanks to his relish in rubbing elbows with dignitaries, he had hosted several joint exhibitions with the Irish embassy and the American embassy in Beijing. I delivered the opening remarks as an emcee for several cocktail parties for his clients and friends. He had also invested in many up-and-coming artists from Spain, Ireland, England, and the US Projects filled up his agenda, so he often worked on an exhibition or a business trip to discover some artists.

Every time I visited his art museum, the palace seemed to have a new glow inside of it. With his careful preservation, many radiant murals on the walls of thousands of years were revived. The gold trims on the silhouette of the palace started to shine again and were especially regal when the sunrays scattered across the space. Dad even combined some East and West elements by dropping a couple of modernist chandeliers from the ceiling and placing a cello at a corner next to one of his traditional Chinese art collections.

Dad took so much pride in growing his art museum in such a prime location. The palace was one of the few ancient architectures left at the heart of the CBD financial district in Beijing. Whenever he took me to one of his business dinners, his friends and clients would tout how successful Dad's art gallery was. "Definitely one of a kind in the art world in Beijing," one of his friends always said.

His art gallery thrived until a year into his divorce with Mom. I heard from Mom that his projects did not come as smoothly as they were before. Dad's temper got even worse as he constantly yelled at his employees if they made the slightest mistakes or, sometimes, for no reason at all. Several of his key staff members resigned because they could not endure his humiliating and scathing criticisms any longer. Gradually, Dad became one lone warrior who tried to run a big art business in a grand palace.

Since the decline of his art business, he rarely attended any events. Mom said he retreated from fighting for his art gallery and started living like a hermit. He still went out a lot because most of the time he was not at home. However, according to my mom, Dad mostly meandered to places with the excuse of "business trips." I could imagine how defeated and depressed he must have felt, especially if he always thought of the glorious past of his art gallery and compared it to what it was like nowadays.

When Dad visited me in Atlanta for graduation, I asked how he was doing with his art business. He assured me there was a "sign of revival" and he was working hard to line up several "big projects." The big words my dad used made me feel how abstract his ideas were, and I knew the more vague his language was, the more likely nothing concrete was on his plate. Seeing my exaggerated nodding, Dad sensed my suspiciousness and frowned. I did not want to probe further into his business, so I stopped asking and accepted what he said as true.

This time when I returned to Beijing, I had a glimpse of the palace several times while Mom drove by. A sea of clients' or visitors' cars used to park in the parking lot next to the palace, but now there were only a couple of them. The gate into the palace used to be wide open with flows of crowds coming in and out for art exhibitions, but now there were no human beings in sight. One time when Mom and I passed by, we noticed the gate was unlocked, so we sneaked inside to see with our own eyes.

The gardens around the palace were still thriving, and the expensive decor, paintings, and artwork were still placed nicely in the museum. Redwood stands and long tables were clean and centered. Chandeliers still bounced off gold sun-rays on the floor like a sea of rare jewels shining, vying for our attention. The only thing missing was life. Silence and stillness filled up the palace and made it feel like a glamorous sleeping dragon. Laughter and chatter from visitors and crowds used to make the palace a lively venue for festivities.

Thousands of years of history came to life when people who were passionate about the arts admired the exquisite artworks and sculpture collections. But all Mom and I could do was recollect the echoes of those memories.

It was an empty palace. I saw so much potential in it yet wondered how it could recover from its stillness if the emperor was gone.

I left Dad's empty gallery hoping one day he would return. Only a couple of staff members took care of the art collections, cleaned the museum daily, and trimmed the gardens outside. Mom did not comment much on my dad's failing business. To me, the palace used to feel like home because it brought a solid sense of security and pride to my family. Now, the emptiness reminds me of the home that is missing.

PART 5

LOST AGAIN

"You cannot let one person destroy your
capacity to love, no?"

CHAPTER 24

Lost Again

———

Though I hated to pull myself away from my mom and grandma again, I was already back in Atlanta after another over seven thousand miles of flight. It was late July, and my graduate program at Duke University would start in less than two weeks.

Kristiaan picked me up from the airport with his suit and tie still on since he'd headed to the airport straight from the office.

The moment we spotted each other among the sea of people at the airport, we started sprinting toward each other. I jumped onto him and he reached out and lifted me in mid-air. Then he started spinning me around in a circle.

"Gosh, I missed you so much! You have no idea." Kristiaan bit my left ear as he whispered.

Then he dragged me out of the airport with my luggage bags and led me to his car. He sped down the highway as if the speed limit did not exist.

The moment we arrived at Kristiaan's apartment, we threw the luggage and backpacks on the floor. Kristiaan picked me up from the floor again and threw me on the bed. We both started panting and could hear each other's racing heartbeats.

Kristiaan gazed at me and untied his tie. He was busy removing all of his unnecessary layers. And then he stood there and took a close look at me, frozen in awe as if he was beholding a heavenly creature. His skin was glowing with the few threads of early evening sunrays beaming through the blinds.

The fact that we both needed to shower no longer seemed significant.

My eyes were fixed on him. Words were inadequate to describe our silent yet boiling love for each other. There was heat from the summer, and then there was heat radiating through our eyes, our hearts, and our breath.

Suddenly, Kristiaan jumped at me and started to unbutton my dress. I felt Kristiaan's passion all over me, so flattering I could not withhold my own any longer. He gently kissed me from head to toe. Then his fingers moved softly on my neck and then slowly around my chest. Every touch made me breathe heavier.

My mind was taken away to another place as I let every inch of Kristiaan's love indulge me. We held each other tightly and moved rhythmically like two Argentine Tango dancers.

We soon lost ourselves in a wonderland that only belonged to us.

***

One week away from the start of my graduate program, I woke up to a regular Tuesday at Kristiaan's apartment. He had already gone to work. My body no longer felt languished or sore from jet lag, although my sense of time was still blurry. I stretched my arms and dragged myself out of bed. Then I marched into the kitchen to cook myself some eggs.

As I munched on my sizzling omelet, my eyes landed on Kristiaan's laptop on his desk. It was unlocked. I did not know if it was my sixth sense, but I wanted to scroll through the photos he saved on his laptop.

It felt wrong obviously to check out his stuff behind his back. But somewhere deep down in my heart, something told me I was about to confront a shocking secret about Kristiaan. I righteously started scrolling through his albums.

What I discovered scarred me for the rest of my life.

Among the photos Kristiaan took of me, there were photos of other girls' legs he took throughout our relationship. From the angle, I could tell that he sneaked around while taking those photos so the girls in his photos would not notice.

A picture is worth a thousand words, and he had loads of pictures.

The dates of the photos helped me connect the dots of Kristiaan's dark secrets that he kept from me for over a year and counting. All this time when we were dating, his eyes had been looking elsewhere.

At first, I felt naive and stupid. How could I not notice any red flags this whole time?

A vile gust of volcanic fury churned from the bottom of my stomach and shot all the way up to the top of my head. I felt utterly betrayed, the same way I felt when I learned about my dad's betrayal of my mom and my family.

The guy I thought was my rock turned out not to be what I believed at all. I wondered how much longer he planned to hide these secrets from me . . . and what other things he was hiding from me.

Suddenly I collapsed on my bed, howling like an injured beast. All my best anticipations about how beautiful my first serious relationship could ever be was shattered. Everything I dreamed about a trusting relationship with Kristiaan got spit on by his lies and secrets. He proved that I was wrong about him.

I thought I would never need to revisit the insecure, painful place where I struggled after my parents' divorce, but here I was again. I had learned more about humiliation and betrayal in the last couple of years than I hoped I would in a lifetime.

This time, the kind of pain that cut through my body was even more deadly. The very person I trusted who could guide me through my dark time was the very person who betrayed me. How cruel was that?

I video called Mom and told her everything. I could barely speak in full sentences because the incessant sobbing almost suffocated me. I felt lost again. Mom was devastated to hear my sorrow and despair, especially because she was on the other side of the world and could not even hug me. She also painfully told me about the tragic correlation between my dad's and Kristiaan's betrayal. "Sadly, that's how some men are," Mom sighed.

Yeah, maybe Mom was right. I'd had enough of feeling betrayed by men and resolved never to rely on others for my happiness again. Kristiaan's betrayal was a wake-up call for me to stop daydreaming about the love stories in the movies or literature but to face reality. It was wishful to think I could trust men after I was proven wrong by my dad and now again by Kristiaan.

Deep down in my memories, I recalled what Mom told me when I was back home: "You cannot let one person destroy your capacity to love, no?"

I promised her I would remember. However, at that moment, it did not make any sense to me. Her words could not save me from feeling heartbroken and lost.

Suddenly, the place where Kristiaan and I spent our time together for the past two years became so hideous. I started destroying anything that reminded me of the beautiful relationship I used to believe in. I aggressively swept the glass-framed photos of Kristiaan and I on my twenty-first birthday onto the floor. My rage almost made me enjoy the distorted satisfaction of hearing the photos shattering into pieces.

Never had I wanted to take off again so badly. I wanted to get away as far as I could to leave all this behind. I wanted to cut him completely from my life.

Kristiaan came back around 6:00 p.m. At first, he was confused by the anger written on my face. It must have looked scary and distorted, a mere reflection of the condemnable mistakes he had made.

"Really? Who do you think you are?" I stared him down, and never had he looked so short, small, and disgusting.

"I don't know what you are talking about." He dared to throw those words at me.

"Don't make me...taking pictures of girls' legs? I feel disgusted when I say it!" I shouted at him like a lion who was about to swallow her prey.

"You looked through my laptop?" Kristiaan acted as if I was in the wrong.

"Don't fucking play this game with me. First, you are a liar, and now you are a coward. You can't even look me in the eye and tell me what you've done!"

My words must have torn him apart. Kristiaan shook all over and collapsed on the floor, not speaking a word.

I just kept staring him down without saying anything either. I let him be crushed by my stare, filled with hatred. He did not dare to look at me because he could not face his own demons.

I started pulling out boxes and packing my things.

"I'm not going to stay here any longer anyway. I am going to Duke, start a new life, and meet new people. You will be long forgotten like a disgusting rat!" I spat those words on him and let him take his own medicine, the kind of humiliation I felt when he made me find out his ugly secrets.

To let me sleep in the bedroom away from him, Kristiaan pulled the air mattress from his closet and curled up into a ball under his blanket in the living room. I began hitting him with pillows until he begged for mercy.

"Now you need mercy? Where was your sense of mercy when you did those things?!"

I spent four hours packing my bags nonstop. My overwhelming grief and anger increased my impressive productivity in packing. They fueled my resolve to break away and cut clean from everything that had Kristiaan in it.

Kristiaan powerlessly lay on his mattress and repeatedly told me to go to bed and get some rest. Ironically, the more he tried to stop me from packing, the more energized I felt. I guess when one experiences profound grief and anger, the energy has to be channeled somehow.

His phone buzzed, and he checked the notification.

"What is it?" I did not know why I still cared at that point.

He did not say anything.

I stood up from the ground and walked past boxes of clothes and books. His eyes were glued to the screen and shame was written all over his face. I took his phone from him and checked his WeChat message—it was from Mom.

It was translated like this:

Both Yaoyao's dad and I are deeply disappointed in you. We thought you loved her with your life, as you said. Mom trusted you, and Yaoyao trusted you. Why did you betray her? You are her first boyfriend, and she has the best anticipations for a pure, devoted, and lasting relationship. You broke her sweetest dream. Mom will let Yaoyao make her decision, but Kristiaan, you surprised our family.

Kristiaan covered his face with his hands, and incessantly whined, "I'm sorry. I'm so sorry..."

"Aside from what you did to me, how could you also break my mom's trust, huh? She's been like a mom to you!" I said, hammering him with my words.

My mom always listened when Kristiaan chatted with her on WeChat about his progress at work or his thoughts on our relationship. He even told her secrets I did not even know. I bet he could not even look her in the eye and confess his mistakes and why he made them.

He also terribly failed my dad. Mom and I chose not to talk about Kristiaan's betrayal of Dad because we had no idea where to begin. It was a miracle Dad gave Kristiaan his approval, and I could only imagine how disheartened he would feel if he knew about Kristiaan's wrongdoing.

How could he?

I tossed his phone on his sad-looking mattress and continued sorting my items neatly in cardboard boxes. Only packing could give me a sense of direction, as it reminded me I would go somewhere else soon. Almost two years of a relationship flashed in front of my eyes. As it played in my mind like a movie, I also tried to mentally burn the tape and erase those memories from my head. Though I wanted to forget about Kristiaan, the bond we had built could not be severed in mere seconds. After all, he was my first boyfriend, and how could two years disappear with the snap of my fingers?

With the special moments Kristiaan and I spent together rewinding in my head, I was not convinced that he did not love me at all. However, he cut me deep and I had no more goodwill left for him. Tears streamed down my face and blurred everything in front of me.

Though it seemed I had a plan to start over in a new place, in reality, I was lost again.

CHAPTER 25

Pushed Into a Downfall Together

———

As much as I wanted to flee from Kristiaan's place the moment I discovered his betrayal, my options were limited. It was the summer after graduation. Most of my friends had already left Atlanta and were back with their families. The few friends who lived in Atlanta were on a graduation trip with their parents. Turning to my friends to sleep on their couch for a few nights was simply not an option.

Besides, I had boxes of items I needed to somehow transport across the state. Shipping them to my new address would be a headache.

Six days left until the move-in date on August 10 to my assigned apartment dorm in Durham, North Carolina. Originally, Kristiaan planned a romantic getaway for us. Our anniversary was around the corner, and he thought there were plenty of vacation spots along the way from Atlanta to Durham. We were supposed to spend about a week in

Savannah, an artsy coastal city built for couples. It would be our chance to spend more time with each other before I relocated. It was meant to be a special escape.

Everything became complicated after the fiasco. Kristiaan booked everything in advance, and it was impossible to cancel last minute, so was the trip still on?

I hadn't spoken to Kristiaan since August 2. I slept on his bed at night, and he was thankful he could even sleep on his air mattress in the living room. Even the thought of being with him in the same space made me want to vomit.

To me, Kristiaan was no more than a stranger occupying the same space as I did. I tried my best to avoid any form of contact with him. No eye contact. No communication. And definitely no physical contact. Whenever Kristiaan tried to lock eyes with me, I could see guilt and a plea for forgiveness written all over his face.

"I would still like to help you move in if you let me." Kristiaan was on his knees with his hands wrapped around my knees. His eyes used to glow with sapphire-blue but were so dull and empty at that moment they gave me chills. I stared down at him and could not speak a word.

"I don't know. I don't want to owe you anything." I asserted myself and wanted to make sure he heard every word clearly.

"No. You don't owe me anything. Helping you move in is the least I could do after all the pain I've caused you..." Kristiaan interrupted me before I could list all the reasons I needed to reject his offer to help.

"Also, if you still want to, I will still take you to Savannah. I think the beach and the artsy town will make you happy," he continued.

My heart cringed when I thought about the tragedy. What was meant to be a romantic getaway for the two of us became a painful and extended period of being together.

"I don't know what to say." All I could think of was misery.

"You don't need to say anything. Just come with me." Kristiaan gazed at me longingly.

Fine. I guess for what our two-year relationship was worth, if the trip would mark the ending, then at least we could make it bittersweet, I thought.

An idiom in Mandarin authentically expressed my mentality, "好聚好散。 (Meet and part on good terms.)"

Kristiaan stood up from the floor and started transferring the boxes into his car downstairs.

***

I was on the passenger seat, looking out of the window at the lush trees passing by.

We were on the highway I-85. Cars sped through the long road that stretched into the horizon. My grief was still too heavy and suffocating for me to hold it all to myself. In need of an outlet, I connected my iPhone to the car. I had more than five hundred songs on my YouTube playlist. I started playing from the first one and made sure the volume was turned up high.

Many lyrics and tunes resonated with my anger, grief, urge for vengeance, and resolve to move on. My voice carried so much weight as I sang along with the music. It was a relieving and almost therapeutic feeling, which made me oblivious to any exhaustion from singing for over four hours straight.

From time to time over the four hours, Kristiaan reached out his right hand and tried to land it on my lap or hold my hand. However, every time, I threw his hand right back at him with disgust. Kristiaan gazed at me many times throughout the long drive. However, I never let him catch my eyes.

"I know that you don't want to talk to me. I want to let you know that your voice is so angelic. Hearing it is a privilege that I do not deserve a bit." Kristiaan turned to me again and locked his eyes on my face. Though I refused to look at him, I could see from my side glimpse that his eyes were red. His eyes used to glow with love and excitement, but now they were filled with anguish, guilt, anger for himself, and endless yearning for my response, even if it meant the slightest trace of acknowledgment of his existence.

"Hah, privilege. I'm singing for myself. It's a shame that somehow you can share it. Breathing the same air with you in this car makes me feel disgusted." I lashed out my anger at Kristiaan. He quickly went silent again. When I howled at him, he jittered like a frightened bunny.

Quaint hotels and artsy stores started to appear on the side of the road. Chic bars and restaurants were tucked in the lush greens by a flowing river. Couples and families floated around in the shades or stopped by the shops like butterflies. A few horse carriages ran through the streets. The iconic Westin resort building overlooking the river convinced me we had arrived in Savannah.

Kristiaan took me to the hotel room he booked for us. We dropped off our stuff, and he asked what I wanted to do. It was around 3:00 p.m. The sky was clear, and the sun was bright. Wholesome weather had a way of inspiring my happy mood, which summoned me to the beach. Kristiaan and I hopped back into the car, and he drove us to Tybee Island.

Late that afternoon, we arrived at Tybee Island, a busy and lively beach town. After I stepped out of the car, I took a deep breath of the salty and refreshing air. My floral sundress twirled as the ocean breeze blew. I looked like a walking bouquet soaking up the sunshine.

Kristiaan bought a beach bag at one of the stores by the coast and stuffed it with beach towels and coconut waters. He knew that coconut water was my favorite.

We walked toward the gold sand beach. I blazed ahead, and Kristiaan skittishly followed. As we got closer, I ran along the shore with bare feet. When I dipped my toes into the sand, I was flattered by the warmth and soft sensation. It felt like a foot massage. Then I sprinted into the water. Ruffled waves pushed toward me. A gush of cool ocean water tingled my feet. It was not cool enough, so I kept running deeper into the water until the waves splashed against my waist.

I closed my eyes. My arms were wide open to embrace the sun, the ocean, and the chirps of the gliding seagulls. I was drenched by the salty and cool water. It seemed to rinse off the toxins that had built up in my body in the past few days. I realized happiness was within my control.

Kristiaan used to tell me that happiness is a choice. When I lost myself in the moment on the beach, I chose to be happy and not think about anything else.

When I looked back, I saw Kristiaan sitting still on a beach towel staring at me. His eyes spoke to his intense yearning to enjoy the moment with me. I looked away immediately to remind him how impossible that was.

When I was tired of playing with the water, I returned to the sand and laid down next to Kristiaan. My eyes fixated on the azure sky. I crossed my arms behind my head and stretched out my legs like a starfish. Seagulls glided above me sporadically. A few toddlers were building sandcastles, and their parents were sunbathing. Clouds floated by in the sky, and sometimes a plane or two appeared. When I closed my eyes, the growling sound of the waves let my mind drift away.

The whole time, Kristiaan stared at me longingly, his eyes filled with guilt.

"You are so beautiful. I just want you to know that I love you," he said cautiously, as if speaking his mind was a crime.

"I don't want to speak to you. I just want to fully enjoy my beach time before you destroy it," I said, immediately rejecting him.

"You feel so far away from me, and I know it's my fault. I've never hated myself this much," he said. "When I look at you, I see everything that I lost."

I did not speak a word. When he realized I had no interest in interacting with him in any way, Kristiaan started checking his phone.

"Who are you texting?" I asked.

"Your mom." Kristiaan kept texting.

"Texting about what? You should not harass her. My mom, Dad, and I are done talking to you. Please fuck off." A cascade of rants flooded out of my mouth.

"I'm sending Mom my apologies. I really want to disappear to cause you less pain. But I love you. I want to..." Kristiaan teared up and started weeping.

Crocodile's tears. I sneered and thought to myself. *Too late. If you know how much pain you'd cause me, then why did you do such a thing in the first place? Save your show for yourself.*

He was used to my silent treatment, but he declared, "I don't know how I will win your trust again, but I'm gonna try my damnedest and give my all and then some. I love you too much to give up."

Several memorable moments happened in the next few days as Kristiaan and I tried to enjoy Savannah while we could.

We went back to Tybee Island a few times, and on the way, rainbows appeared out of the blue. When Kristiaan and I spotted the rainbows, we both appreciated how lucky we were. I never thought I could feel lucky after Kristiaan's betrayal. Those rainbows restored some hope and positive energy in me.

Kristiaan also took me on a dolphin watching tour. Many dolphins jumped among the waves and followed us closely by the tail of the boat. Watching them swimming in the ocean gleefully set my mind free. I wished I was one of the dolphins, playing in the ocean without any worries.

It was hard to dwell on past grudges when Kristiaan and I both indulged in the moment. Traveling together brought us a bit closer since the day I broke up with him. We often created blithe memories. I had done that with him for two years. It almost made me believe I could still feel happy around him, even though I knew deep down it was wishful yet beautiful thinking.

One evening when we chilled by the beach again, I stood up and noticed the sun had started setting. The sun fired up the entire sky. Clouds were painted in the colors of strawberry vanilla ice cream. As the sun slowly dropped beneath the horizon, the view seemed to send me a message.

"It's the end of a chapter in my life. Tomorrow starts a new chapter," I whispered.

***

Kristiaan struggled to lift many heavy boxes into my new dorm. We had finally made it to Durham and started to set everything up for my new place. Kristiaan unpacked and assembled the furniture and accessories for my room. He said it was important to create a homey space I could feel excited to return to at the end of each day.

Though I had my best anticipations for the new chapter in my life, the reality turned out to be quite contrary to what I had hoped for. Throughout the next few months in the graduate program, many unfortunate events piled up that pushed me to several mental breakdowns.

When I was all alone again, I experienced many sleepless nights when the trauma haunted me. I still had so many questions as to why he lied to me, and how he could betray and hurt me. Nothing really made sense. This nonsense kept me awake at night along with the mounting stress from my intense coursework and roommate problems.

One day in early September, Kristiaan called me, crying like a baby, and said, "My firm is experiencing a crisis due to a person who committed fraud. Now it is a shitshow with lawsuits...Apparently, everyone is affected."

I knew exactly what he meant. He was going under, together with the big ship that he was on board.

Everything was sinking. My life, my sanity, my well-being, and his life, his sanity, and his well-being.

Life threw us into an abyss like a beast with its mouth open, trying to eat us alive. I was free-falling into despair, anger, sadness, endless stress, and mental breakdowns. No matter how much I fought, gravity only pulled me downward closer to the hungry monster.

Completely out of control, Kristiaan and I were pushed into a catastrophic downfall. Little did I know this would bring us together again.

CHAPTER 26

Driving Around the World for a Second Chance

———

The stress and overwhelming workload in my graduate program had already created a challenging lifestyle for me—many sleepless nights, mental breakdowns, and hectic schedules that never seemed to end. My roommate continued destroying the only place where I could hide at the end of the day. Roaches were crawling all over the kitchen, and the apartment smelled like rotten dead bodies. After contacting housing for weeks with no reply, I totally lost hope in the possibility that the housing staff would do their job and my circumstances would get better at all.

Since the day Kristiaan helped me move into my dorm in Durham, he had been driving six hours each way every weekend to see me. From Atlanta to Durham one way was about 380 miles. No matter if he got off work late on Friday nights, or there were accidents on the highway or thunderstorms flooding the roads, he always showed up at my door no matter what.

At first, I insisted he should not come; the last person I wanted to see was him. It was hard not to be constantly reminded of the trauma inflicted by Kristiaan if I had to face him standing in front of me. However, Kristiaan did not listen but came to visit me every weekend, without any exceptions.

"Why are you here?" I shouted at Kristiaan once when he showed up in front of my door again.

"I'm worried about you. I know you hate me and don't want to see me, but I want to be right next to you when you are trying to heal."

Some days, I would throw temper tantrums, yelling and throwing pillows at him. But others, I just let him try to make me happier. The weekends became the only time of the week when I could breathe some fresh air in the mountains at Asheville, North Carolina, or have fun playing mini golf with Kristiaan.

Over our anniversary weekend, he took me on another special trip to Asheville, where we saw a baby black bear by the road. It evoked many of my memories when Kristiaan and I spotted fortunate signs such as the rainbows and dolphins we saw on Tybee Island.

Kristiaan knew that watching the sunset was one of my favorite activities. He booked a table by the window at a restaurant on the top floor of a mountain-view resort. It was located on the top of a hill, nuzzled in the tranquil landscape, overlooking the west side of the sky.

While we munched on the lobsters and oysters, Kristiaan asked, "How are you feeling?"

With my lobster in mid-bite, I looked out of the window to see the flaming sunset, turned my head back, and gazed at him. "I feel calm. A lot has been going on in my head these past few days. I've never felt myself growing up so rapidly."

"I'm happy that you feel calm."

"I don't know what will happen, but unlike before, I look forward to what's to come," I said softly yet confidently as Kristiaan gazed at my face reflecting the radiant colors of the sunset.

For the first time since Kristiaan broke my heart, a sense of balance and peace was restored in me.

From late summer when the weather had just started to turn chilly, to autumn when leaves were falling like rain, until the brutally cold winter when the wind was howling, Kristiaan never missed one weekend to come and be with me. Before he left each Monday, he always made sure I had all the groceries I needed for the week. Sometimes when I was cramming for eight-thousand-word final papers, Kristiaan was the one who put dinner on my desk and powered me through the long night of writing. He gave me neck massages and made sure to proofread the whole paper before he went to sleep around 4:00 a.m.

Kristiaan had his own problems to solve, dealing with the FBI's investigation of the fraud conducted by an employee at his firm. As an executive, he also took on the responsibility of saving the firm and tried to rebuild the business from the ruins. Despite his thorny situation, Kristiaan chose to support me in any way he could.

He was also there to help me deal with the frustrations of my living situation. Though it was never his burden to bear, he helped me take out the trash and clean the apartment to make my living space just a little more comfortable despite my roommate's indecency and utter irresponsibility.

Kristiaan's wrongdoing in the past still ached my heart occasionally or crept into my nightmares by surprise. He had been trying with all his effort to become a rock on which I could depend. He had been proving with his actions that he meant every word when he told me at Tybee Island that he was determined to be with me and would give his all and then some to win my trust again.

One day, toward the end of the semester, when final exams approached, Kristiaan and I realized that the mileage on his car suggested he had driven over twenty-five thousand miles to visit me since the first weekend he drove from Atlanta up to Durham. Twenty-five thousand miles is about the length of the equator.

Mom said Kristiaan supported me like a family member, and even she would find it challenging to convince herself to drive twelve hours every weekend just to see me. Kristiaan's persistent efforts to repent and his love for me made me believe he might have a chance to rebuild our broken relationship.

He was driving around the world to see me and try to make me happy, even if that meant spending less than forty-eight hours with me every week.

***

Among all the chaos, another underlying time bomb was about to explode. This one was about my performance in the graduate program. My mounting mental health issues were largely engendered by stressors such as injustice from housing's decisions, pressure from coursework, and recurring pain from Kristiaan's betrayal. Instead of helping me out with my roommate situation, the housing department moved me into another dorm, in the middle of my hectic week, all within twenty-four hours.

There was no way I could pack all my belongings into boxes and move them into a new dorm in a few hours, even if I did not sleep. I had no time to cry about the unjust decision. Out of despair, I called Kristiaan, who drove overnight and helped me settle into my new apartment. He left the next day because he still had to work.

I felt like I was putting out a wildfire that raged ever more viciously by the day. One day, the program director broke the news that I was on the brink of not meeting the requirements, which could risk my status in the program.

This time, I could not take it anymore.

I did not go to class for days, not answering emails or phone calls from anyone. I curled up in my bed and wrapped myself in my soft comforter, the only thing that could make me feel safe—just like the last time when my world fell apart after my mom told me the news about the divorce.

Kristiaan called me many times. He first tried the phone but in vain because I turned it off. Then he video called me on Facebook, but I shut down my laptop as well. I ignored all of his calls.

One day, campus police visited my dorm to do a security check to make sure I was still alive. They said Kristiaan called them to see if I was okay and he was on his way here.

I glossed over my situation to the campus police just so I could return to my bed.

In my enclosed space, it was easy to lose the sense of time. There was no light, no life, only deadly silence. I started to destroy anything within my reach. The kitchenware, the vases, the glass bottles were all shattered everywhere on the floor. At one point, I picked up a piece of glass shard from the ground and held it right next to my wrist. I was that close to hurting myself.

What's the point of living if I can't see a purpose? If the system is against me, if the world seems so evil, do I even want to be part of it? Such thoughts ran through my mind.

Tired of breaking things, I passed out in despair.

God knows when Kristiaan arrived at my place. When I woke up to loud knocks on the door, it was already midnight. When I opened the door, he looked absolutely exhausted, his clothes drenched in sweat and his eyes shaded by dark circles.

He rushed toward me and enclosed me in his arms, "Gosh, why did you not answer my calls? Your mom and I were worried sick!"

I let out a heart-wrenching cry, unable to speak a word. Words could not describe the fatigue, hopelessness, and despair I felt after these series of unjust events hit me like bricks, nonstop.

Kristiaan canceled his work schedule and stayed with me until the very last day of the semester to make sure I would not think about hurting myself again. He took me to places where I could take my mind off my problems, such as the gardens or the mountains. He even helped me with my endless assignments. He prepared food before my exams and walked me to the door of the exam room just to tell me I could do it. He saved me from my worst nightmares and suicidal thoughts.

My mom and I were so grateful to Kristiaan for showing up at a time when I needed him most.

"No matter what mistakes he made before, he was there when you were about to hurt yourself. He saved your life! I will be forever grateful for that," Mom said on a video chat.

When I told Kristiaan how much I appreciated that he dropped everything in his life just to be with me, he said the same line as usual: "I needed to make sure you are safe. It's the least I could do."

Kristiaan's actions proved his unwavering love for me and how much he was determined to change for the better, not only for himself but for both of us. When Kristiaan drove me back to Atlanta after final exams, I said, "I think I want to give you a second chance."

He looked surprised, as if he could not believe what he heard. I thought it was time for me to let go of the past that kept haunting me, see through the ups and downs in my relationship with Kristiaan, and appreciate what he had done since the day I discovered his flaws. Had Kristiaan not loved me at all, why would he overcome all the troubles to be with me and help me regardless of the hardship in his life?

"One person cannot destroy your capacity to love, no?" Mom's words emerged in my mind again. They started to make sense to me now that I had more experience. Kristiaan showed me that nothing could stop him from loving me, and he would do anything to rebuild our trust and love.

Deep down, I knew I loved him all along. Had I not cared about my relationship at all with Kristiaan, why was I in so much pain?

"I will try to win your heart back every day. I will show you that choosing me is not a mistake." Kristiaan looked at me while his hands were on the steering wheel.

"I will see to that. My parents will see to that."

"Yes, you *will* see." He grinned with conviction.

As I stared at the road ahead, which stretched into the distance as if it would never end, I zoned out. When I thought about my bumpy life over the past few months, a voice inside my head said it was time to stop and end this vicious cycle for good.

I wanted a second chance as well. I was tired of suffering any longer and decided to reset my life. Though I did not know where to begin, I knew I wanted to find out with Kristiaan beside me.

CHAPTER 27

Following My Wanderlust

———

Winter 2019 in Atlanta was dry and dull. Besides the bone-chilling cold, there was nothing else—not even a single snowflake—that could make me feel the magic of the season. The climate reflected the state of my life in an uncannily suggestive way. Nothing much was going on with me, except feeling stuck and miserable. I let the days in late December flee by on my calendar. During the day, I spent hours pondering what I should do with my life.

At the end of my chaotic time in the graduate program, it was time to take a break and dive deep into myself to figure out what my next steps were. I decided to stop wasting more time and drop from the program that did not seem to be a good fit for me. So I moved back to Atlanta with Kristiaan.

Kristiaan suffered from the distress of trying to revive his crumbled firm. He was normally a laid-back person, but during this time, he could be quite querulous. Some days when he returned home, he locked himself in his room and didn't come out for hours. The conflict between him and I was brewing. Over time, I had less patience and tolerance for him, and we had many late-night fights.

In the meantime, the outbreak of Covid-19 took place in China. Watching the news every day about the staggering figures of death made me want to go back to Mom and Grandma to power through the alarming time with them.

"Yaoyao, how are you doing?" Mom video called me on the first day of 2020.

"Mom, how are YOU doing? How about my grandma?" I asked impatiently in Mandarin and hoped that everyone was healthy and well.

"We are fine. We are quarantined and can't go anywhere. The toughest part is that for the Spring Festival this year, we are not allowed to visit relatives or have group gatherings anymore." Mom looked sad and exhausted.

The Spring Festival is one of the most important holidays in China, and every year, families celebrate and welcome the spring together. However, Covid-19 impeded many people from returning home to their families. The Spring Festival had never been so quiet before.

"Mom, I want to come back home to be with you and Grandma. Honestly, things are not going well with me..." I burst out into tears as I shared my grievances with my mom.

"No, I want you to be safe. Airports are one of the most dangerous places you could be right now. The virus is so lethal, and you have no idea. Besides, once you come back, you will be instantly quarantined in a hotel for two weeks—alone in your own room without seeing anyone!" Mom raised her voice as she tried to emphasize the dire situation.

I started sobbing. Guilt and helplessness erupted in my mind. I felt so ashamed that I could not be with my family when they were battling a pandemic that had killed thousands of people. I could not be further away from my home, given that I was on the other side of the globe.

"Mom, but... please be cautious. Please stay healthy with Grandma. Wear your masks and try not to go out except to get groceries." The least I could do was remind Mom to take extra care.

"We will be fine. You take care of yourself. And don't think about stupid thoughts again. I was so devastated. You have no idea. How could you even think something like that? I would kill myself if something happened to you, you know that?" Mom started sobbing as well when she recalled the gut-wrenching scene of me collapsing on the floor among the shards of sharp objects in my dorm in Durham.

Though I could not hug Mom to tell her everything would be okay, I assured her I would stay strong in this challenging time, with her, together.

***

On January 3, after reflecting upon the past few months of my life, I decided to no longer allow myself to sink deeper into my misery. I had enough of sleepless nights when I was haunted by my past and nightmares. I had enough of crying my heart out in search of the answers to life's problems. I had enough of getting stuck in a place where I could not escape from and in a complicated relationship that did not go anywhere. Something drastic had to happen in my life to start a major reboot.

I remembered when I decided to solo travel to Israel and the spring when I booked a one-way plane ticket to Dubai. It occurred to me that whenever I was at a crossroads in my life, my wanderlust guided me to explore the world on my own to get myself unstuck.

The virus had not reached the rest of the world yet, so I sat down in front of my laptop and browsed through Conde Nast Travel, Travel + Leisure, and other sites that could offer me some inspiration. After hours of researching ideas, the Caribbean kept showing up on my screen and gripping my attention.

The islands in the Caribbean such as the Bahamas were always on my mind or on the tip of my tongue. Somehow, I'd never actually booked a one-way flight to spend my vacation there. This time nothing would stop me, and my mind was set on going. I quickly opened up several tabs on my browser that showed me flight options, hotels, and must-dos. Enticing visuals of the secluded islands, the pink sand beach, the swimming pigs, and the tropical sunshine all year round filled me with excitement. My heart pounded faster as I discovered more adventure ideas. The islands were calling!

I started planning my solo travels in the Caribbean around noon. However, by the time I finally tried to narrow down my focus and was almost ready to book the details, the sun was setting on the horizon.

Thanks to my thorough research, I locked in a few great deals on flights and hotels. I planned to stay in the Bahamas for nine days, and then nine days in Turks and Caicos. After that, my island-hopping plans were up in the air. I simply left the rest as a mystery that would unfold along my journey.

I clicked "reserve" a few times. Done!

Kristiaan only knew about my travel plans after my plan was set in stone. Though he had full confidence in my experience in solo traveling, he was still worried about my safety. He turned on his laptop and looked up a few areas in Nassau where assaults on tourists had been reported. To make sure I kept this information in mind, Kristiaan wrote down the names of the areas in a notebook, and he even drew a map in case I was unaware of the location.

Jumping out of my chair, I stepped onto the balcony. The evening still had a few remaining golden threads of sunshine that painted one corner of the sky in rose gold, pearl pink, and some flame red. I took a deep breath and let the invigorating energy lift my spirit.

I saw in front of me the colors of hope, anticipation, and a new beginning. I could not wait to fly away and let wanderlust take me to where my heart desired.

CHAPTER 28

The Bahamas

———

Swimming pigs are such darlings of the Bahamas that whenever they show up on big advertising boards at the airports, people instantly know that the islands of the Bahamas are summoning their visits.

Given the volatile weather in the past few days, I was thankful that it was sunny, though the sea was slightly rough, but it was okay to set sail to Rose Island.

The moment I dipped my toes into the sand, my excited mind quieted down and was in sync with the ocean breeze.

The island cheered me up because it showed me what I love. I loved immersing myself in nature and being part of it. The beauty of nature—the ocean, the sky, the lush greens, the creatures—connected with me and made me feel alive. The island provided me with the space to breathe and think about my dreams. My inner artist was activated by the island vibe and my creative expressions started to flow. I naturally felt I belonged to the space where I could relax and think about becoming a writer or building my own media brand inspired by my intense wanderlust and curiosity for the world.

Around lunchtime, three loud and snorting pigs marched from the bush and stepped into the white sand. One pig had ginger red hair throughout. Another had milky white as the primary color and some chocolate spots scattered throughout its body. The last one reflected baby pink on its skin.

They trotted toward the shore and dipped their feet in the water. In the beginning, they meandered around aimlessly. After they rinsed off the dust and sand between their toes, they started swimming into the waves. Their heads were above the water, tilting up into the sky. Their mouths looked naturally arched, such that it seemed like they kept smiling cheek to cheek.

My eyes locked on the merry swimming pigs, and I wished I was one of them. Everyone on the beach was attracted to these carefree, adorable animals.

The swimming pigs changed my perception about pigs in the farms that are wrapped in mud and shit. I was amused by what I saw. Another counterintuitive trait about those pigs was that they were surprisingly agile in the water. They swam so swiftly like powerboats in the sea, defying the stereotype of pigs being lazy and slow.

Some locals brought food and gestured for the pigs to come back to the shore.

"Could you give me some food for the pigs? I'd like to feed them as well," I asked one of the locals.

"Sure. Open your palm flat and let the pigs come to you." He gave me a few tips on how to have a fun time with the pigs.

I squatted and extended out my arm with my palm facing up. The pig with ginger red hair trotted toward me with its hair flopping up and down joyfully. At first, I feared it would run over me with its great excitement for the food. However, it slowed down when its nose touched my fingers. It snorted and took the food from my hand. Hearing it chew so loudly even made me feel hungry. I decided to enjoy my meals as contently as these pigs. They always seemed so content and jovial. I believe their attitude was shaped by the nonchalant island vibe.

After I returned to my hotel room, I started scrolling through the hundreds of photos I had taken in the past few days to relive the memories. I learned to relax and let things be while I was on the islands. That night I had a dream in which I heard a voice echoing from the heart of the island saying, "Enjoy the present. Everything is going to be okay."

***

Unfortunately, your excursion to Eleuthera and Harbour Island is canceled due to rough seas. The next trip will not resume until further notice.

Seriously? I woke up to another 7:00 a.m. email giving me bad news on the day I was supposed to sunbathe on the pink sand beach and walk through a cave by the cove. My plans were ruined two days in a row now. The worst part was that I did not know until the last minute.

Instead of wasting time on whining and complaining about the weather, I quickly formed a backup plan with the help of the concierge and signed up for an exciting dolphin experience.

I had never had a close-up encounter with dolphins before. Most of the time I saw them in dolphin shows, and the closest I had ever been to them was through a glass wall at the aquarium. When I knew I had the opportunity to swim with them, I was ecstatic.

My longing for the sea started when I was little, and I formed a special connection with the wonders of marine life. The ocean kept appearing in my dreams and summoned my incessant curiosity with its mysterious aura. Under the deep blue, there exists a totally different yet bustling world where animals of all kinds thrive—blue whales, white sharks, dolphins, manta rays, sea turtles, and so much more. Having the honor of integrating myself into their world had always been my dream. Home is where I feel free, excited, relaxed, and most in sync with myself. Animals, especially sea creatures, made me feel at home. I believed if I could swim like a fish or float like a jellyfish, I would be in my natural habitat.

Thinking of my childhood ocean memories, I hopped on the boat that took me to Blue Lagoon where I would go swimming with the dolphins.

"Hello! I'm your instructor, Rico. Are you ready to dive in with the dolphins?" A tall and energetic guy in his early thirties walked toward me and gave me a high five. His skin was dark tan but had a special glow that you could only get from being in the ocean for a long time.

"I'm Mary. I am so thrilled to be here." Though I had my wetsuit on, my voice was shaking when I put my legs into the chilly water.

"Hello! I'm Danielle and this is my husband Tony." A couple celebrating their anniversary from Connecticut joined me as well.

"Nice to meet you both. Pretty exciting, huh?" I tried to smile back at them and hid my fear of the cold water.

"I can see that your legs are shivering. The best thing to do is to dive in with one jump!" Danielle could see my discomfort with the cold, and I bet she could also see I'd been spoiled in the Southern weather for the past five years.

"You guys are lucky! Usually, there are at least ten people in a group. Today you are going to have some VIP time with the dolphins." After Rico gave a brief instruction on where not to touch the dolphins, he made us feel extra special.

Tony and Danielle leaped into the water and turned back around to whistle for me to hurry up. They laughed when I flopped into the cold water with a sharp squeak. Rico told us the dolphin who would play with us was called Princess.

She was muscular and gorgeous. Her curves were pronounced, and she always had a frisky expression. At first, she swam in front of us with her belly up. We had the privilege of touching her silky body. When I reached out and felt her skin, it was slick and soft like jelly.

Princess gave me a big hug with her side fins resting on my shoulders and her head pressed against mine. She always made a crisp, high-pitched, and joyful sound when she interacted with me. Sometimes I could see her clean and shining teeth when she opened her mouth as if to smile.

I felt closer to Princess by the minute as we played with each other in the water. When Princess pushed my feet and rushed forward for a surfing position, we had fun like friends. Although we could not communicate with each other, our gestures, expressions, and feelings could translate despite our differences.

Later, two male dolphins, Stormy and Paul, joined our festivities. Their bodies seemed more edgy, whereas Princess showed off her curves to the world. When Stormy and Paul both pushed me around swiftly through the water surface, I felt a surge of adrenaline. With water splashing on the side of my face, I could hardly see where these two strong boys steered me. The dolphins and I built an unspeakable trust. After a while, I no longer worried about rushing to different directions blindfolded but started to surrender to the amazing trust I had with Stormy and Paul. A rush of intense elation flooded through my body as I flew on the water surface with the dolphins. That long afternoon playing with dolphins in the ocean made me feel at home. It reminded me of how I ran around on the beach with my parents when I was a five-year-old.

Just when I wanted more fun with the dolphins, it was about time for me to return to the boat and head back. Princess, Stormy, and Paul gave me affectionate kisses on my lips and cheeks. Stormy even made a joke by showing off his tongue, as if he was saying, "I want more! French kiss!"

I was crestfallen about saying goodbye to my dolphin friends. On the boat ride back, Danielle and Tony chatted with me about the experience.

"It's truly amazing, isn't it?" Danielle asked as she sat next to me.

"Absolutely. Where are you going next?" I was curious about the couple's plans.

"No more destinations for us! Our vacation is over. We will fly out tomorrow morning. Not ready for the cold," Tony lamented.

"Definitely not looking forward to returning to the real world." Danielle sighed and looked into the distance.

"The good time is always so short. It's a nice escape for us, without the kids, work, or any responsibilities," Tony continued.

Danielle and Tony elicited my own thought about stealing time from the real world to escape once or twice. Solo travels allowed me to take my mind off my compounding problems. Having a getaway sporadically allowed me to reflect, rewind, and recuperate. I thought about how my time in Israel helped me learn about independence as a young adult, and how my time in Italy taught me about trust and family. Each of my adventures brought me closer to myself and my sense of home and belonging.

I also realized travel plans do not always pan out, but I managed to have a great time in the end.

When the sun went down and the night came out, I sat in my room lit by a dim reading light. I put my conch shell that I found on the island in the middle of the table and stared at its baby pink color and ocean glow. The whole day at Blue Lagoon Island and my magical time with the dolphins replayed in front of me like a movie.

***

Locals say the Bahamas are sunny 365 days a year. I believe them. And perhaps that is the secret reason why people living here always seem to be so happy, radiating smiles that reflect the sun.

"Welcome everyone! I'm your captain, Christopher. Today we have awesome weather to go snorkeling at the three reefs." The captain described our agenda. "The first one is where the scene of Johnny Depp getting stranded in the *Pirates of the Caribbean* is filmed. At the second and the third snorkeling sites, you will have the chance to spot sea turtles and reef sharks!"

"We don't want to lose a leg or an arm when we are snorkeling at the third reef!" Some folks responded, half joking.

"Don't worry. We will make sure you come back in one piece!" The captain chuckled.

Without further ado, the captain sat in position and steered the boat into the blue ocean. Soon the boat started to pick up speed. I sat toward the end corner of the boat, looking at the white-water splash pushing against the boat and contrasting with the shades of blue. The salty ocean breeze tingled my face. Looking around, I saw the colors of the water intertwine and stretch into the horizon.

My time in the Bahamas suddenly felt so short when the last day arrived. All the days before that, I dallied, and my island life seemed to last forever.

A few more waves later, we anchored at our first snorkeling site.

I put on a life jacket and snorkeling gear and stepped into a pair of fins. While standing next to the edge of the boat, I was not sure if I was ready to dive into the deep blue, filled with curious creatures, wonders, and even dangerous uncertainties. My only source of courage came from the giant sun in the sky, warming everything beneath. The water was crystal clear, and I could already see sea fans, fish of different sizes, and corals.

I took a huge leap forward, jumping into the magnificent world of wonder. When my skin was embraced by the cool ocean water, my body felt the instant refreshing sensation, a bit too intense at first but quickly offset by the warm sunshine and the soothing ocean. The first few seconds of anxiety and shock quickly transformed into indulgence in the natural sea salt spa. When I embraced the turquoise Atlantic water, all my worries and nerves vanished in the air, carried away by the soft ocean breeze. I put my head down and started exploring the magical world under the water.

Through my goggles, I saw the calm and busy marine life thriving and meandering around me. Corals rooted themselves on the seabed, radiating their dazzling colors of coral pink, sandy brown, and, sometimes, verdant green. Sea fans danced with the currents, flowing with schools of fish. It was marvelous to see the vibrant colors reflected from the fish scales, resembling a mosaic of hidden gems shining from the bottom of the deep blue.

Some of the fish were bigger than my head, swimming above the corals and taking their time, like cops patrolling the traffic. Others were as small as Nemo, coming in and out of the corals as if the world was too dangerous for them to explore. I was especially amused when I saw the Caribbean's famous parrotfish, which had a dramatic collection of colors—bright yellow mixed with neon green. Its lips were comically bloated, making the parrotfish look like a sexy and desperate kisser.

I kept swimming and following a medley of creatures telling their stories.

When I hopped back onto the boat, everyone shared the amazing world they discovered underwater. Their excitement was glowing just like the corals and fish I spotted.

When we arrived at the second reef, I was the first person to dive into the water. As I floated around aimlessly, a sea turtle appeared beneath my belly. The sea turtle swam forward, with its fins swinging up and down like a bird. It took its time without a set schedule, a known destination, or any peer pressure. The turtle was all by itself enjoying its surroundings just like me. All the wonders I had the privilege to witness so far made me feel like one of the sea creatures, cohabiting with these numerous species. In a weird yet amazing way, I felt like I belonged—the boundless sea world became my home where all my worries were washed away, where I could simply be happy and take everything in. Nothing bad could ever happen.

Our sea salt spa day ended with snorkeling at the last reef, which was the most thrilling among all. We had the chance to get up close and personal with reef sharks!

The captain said reef sharks were not interested in humans, but their looks still gave us chills.

The water was colder than before, adding a bit more emotional tension as I felt my heart pounding fast again. The intense chilliness matched the environment where the sharks liked to play. As I looked intently through my goggles searching for any signs of reef sharks, one big grey shark approached me from behind. It first tapped my feet and then swam under my belly, swiftly moving forward with its tail steering its way. When I saw its full body, it took a deep dive and disappeared into the dark blue abyss. The whole experience was so intimate yet intimidating that I still could not wrap my head around the fact that a shark could get so close to me casually. My silent and hair-raising encounter with the reef shark was beyond words.

On the boat ride back to the shore, I could not stop thinking about how lucky and grateful I was to witness and be a part of this amazing ocean. The beauty, colors, and wonder, mixed with a tinge of danger, stirred up my senses and kept me in awe. My skin was exposed in the sun, and I watched drops of sea salt crystalize on my arms and legs. My joy and overwhelming happiness reminded me of the place where I could feel at home, where I could float freely in the turquoise hue.

CHAPTER 29

Turks and Caicos

———

I needed a refreshing break so I could return with an invigorated mindset and rested body.

When I left my daily struggles and uneventful life back in Atlanta to go island-hopping, I wasn't sure what I would get out of this trip. I felt called to go on it, but I didn't know why. I knew it would be relaxing, it would de-stress me, and I'd have fun on various adventures, but only when I was actually there, did I realize the real reason I needed to go.

The first step to lead an exciting life was to switch into a positive mindset. I had strayed so far from that mentality, and my depression had led me on a downward spiral. The feeling of betrayal from my parents and boyfriend, my roommate issues, my hefty load of classwork, and my sense of utter despair when I looked at my pile of problems had sucked me into a dark place I needed to get out of.

On top of that, I left Atlanta worried about the ongoing tension between Kristiaan and I due to his issues at work and concern for my family in Beijing, who were under quarantine because of COVID-19. Many times, my conflicts with Kristiaan escalated into long-night fights, which made me scream, "I can't do this anymore!" I wanted to leave, but I had nowhere else to go. The furthest I could be away from Kristiaan was sleeping upstairs on the couch, even when he begged me to sleep with him in the same bed. As a solo traveler, I hated feeling stuck in a situation from which I struggled to escape.

Stressing about all of this wasn't helping. It was only bringing me down further. When I focused on the problems in my daily life, I felt depressed and exhausted.

I learned during my stay in the Bahamas that I could reset my mind to think more positively. Although many of my excursions were unexpectedly canceled due to the weather, instead of whining about my bad luck, I learned to adapt and came up with new plans to enrich my day. My solo travels were full of surprises and spontaneity, which gradually enhanced my patience and shaped me as a person who embraces uncertainties. This was the beginning of a mental shift in the right direction. Soon, this mindset would lead me to better handle the stresses of daily life back home.

But it wasn't the only thing I learned on this trip. I would have another realization about love.

***

"To really feel the island vibe, stay in the Turks and Caicos," one of my taxi drivers in Nassau said. He said the Bahamas was commercialized compared to Turks, and much of the island was pristine and untouched there.

The driver's advice convinced me to book my flight and resort and explore Turks and Caicos for nine days. I hopped onto an InterCaribbean flight on a sunny Wednesday, February 12, two days before Valentine's Day. The holiday designed for couples to celebrate their love made me daydream about my own love.

While I was sitting by a window seat overlooking the Caribbean turquoise waters from above, I thought about Kristiaan. I knew, at the end of my island adventures, Kristiaan would be waiting for me to return to his arms. We would get through this challenging time together, as we had been. I felt a rushing wave of hope wash over me. It would all be okay, and I felt a new lifestyle was waiting for me to unlock it.

I could not wait to see what my solo adventures at Turks and Caicos would teach me as well.

***

It was a short thirty-minute flight. When I landed in Providenciales, no tall constructions were in sight. The taxi driver was right—I could experience the authentic island here.

My resort was tucked in a lush botanical garden. The moment I stepped into the space, a Zen vibe calmed my senses. A pool at the center of the resort was surrounded by bamboos, orchids, and other plants. Stone mini sculptures and pebbles were decorated across the resort. I found my room under a massive plumeria flower tree. It covered my place in shades like a giant umbrella. A couple of wind chimes were hanging on the tree. When the island breeze slipped through the tree, a melodious sound echoed in the air and carried me away in an island dream.

My brain was wired to the ocean during my days on the island. My first impulse after dropping off my luggage in my room was to get right back to the beach. I changed into my bikini and wrapped a large scarf around my body. Then I flip-flopped my way to the shore.

Provo was less crowded than the Bahamas. As my butler told me, Provo was all about the water. Boating, yachting, paragliding, and cruising to scattered islands around North and Middle Caicos were only some of the ways one might enjoy Turks. Instead of seeking something to do to keep myself on the move, I lay down on a beach chair to bask in the sun. Almost as soon as I closed my eyes and stretched my arms and legs out like a starfish, my mind drifted away.

I woke up again about two hours later. After my luxurious nap, my adventurous spirit summoned me to try something thrilling. A boat with a parachute approached the shore, so I spontaneously decided to try parasailing. The captain attached me firmly to the parachute, and when he sped up the boat, I took off right away. I floated in the air and was rapidly elevated among the clouds. A few seagulls glided in the sky, and I felt as if I was one of them. The cool, salty air woke up my senses, and I savored the rush of the breeze at the high altitude.

Over the next few days, I kept my high spirits and explored Iguana and Half Moon Bay, North and Middle Caicos, Long Bay, and Grand Turks.

I took a speed boat to Iguana Island and Half Moon Bay. The captain took me and a few other travelers to the middle of the ocean and let us snorkel, free as the fish. As soon as I embraced the astonishing aquamarine hue again, electrifying excitement ran through my body. During the trip, I made some new friends—a mom and her daughter who were on vacation. We quickly turned into travel and photo buddies. When we dipped our toes into the sands on Iguana Island, a group of iguanas popped out of the bushes. They seemed well-fed and not scared of humans at all. Then we ventured onto the other side of the island to climb a dark reef. We marveled at the calm and beautiful view of the sunset on the beach.

Though I was having so much fun swimming among the waves and taking photos with my new friends, they reminded me of my own loved ones. I thought of Mom, Grandma, and Kristiaan. I wished they could be here with me to enjoy these wonderful moments together. Without the support of my family, I would not have the opportunity to travel wherever my heart took me. My freedom to soul search in various places in the world was indebted to my family's sacrifice. "Sacrifice is part of love." I thought of how Mom told me to appreciate the lifestyle I had. "Don't complain too much. Think about what you have and show gratitude," she would say.

My heart cringed when I recalled the unappreciative words that slipped out of my mouth when I traveled with my mom in Amsterdam two summers ago. When I was frustrated with my challenges after my parents' divorce, I lashed out, "Life would be much easier if I'd been born in a different family!" As I soaked up the sun on the island, I was glad I had become more grateful for my family, who provided me with the means to embark on my healing journey. Exploring parts of the globe on my own gave me ample time to reflect on my changes in attitude. I planted a seed in my heart to one day take my family on a luxurious vacation to the places I had been.

Mom's reminder also made me contemplate my relationship with Kristiaan. Perhaps it was time to put myself in his shoes and try to understand the considerable amount of stress he had to cope with while rebuilding a firm from the ground up. If I could be more understanding of his situation, we might have fewer conflicts that would be replaced by sympathy.

Love is a funny thing, isn't it? I thought. *When it is around me all the time, I start to lose sight of how much joy it brings me. Now that I am away from my family, I miss them so much.*

On Valentine's Day, just when I picked up my phone to dial Kristiaan's number, he called me.

"Happy Valentine's, sweetheart. I miss you so much!" Kristiaan said.

"Me too." My voice was soft and slow. I was lost in my thoughts of love and happiness.

"What fun stuff did you do today?" he asked, interrupting my thoughts.

"I cruised out to the islands in North and Middle Caicos. It was a small group. Only eight people. We spotted humpback whales breaching, snorkeled around some uninhabited islands, and had fresh conch salad made from the conchs we collected straight from the ocean. And for the first time, I saw flying fish with my own eyes." I felt excited again just by reliving my adventures.

"Wow, I'm so glad you had fun." Kristiaan sounded jealous.

"You know, I really wish you were here." I lowered my voice, thinking it would be the first Valentine's that Kristiaan and I could not spend together. I knew he had to take care of his work to get his firm's business back on track.

"Trust me, I want to be there with you too sweetheart, but I have so much to take care of, for both of us." He sighed.

"I know. Don't push yourself too hard. I love you."

I remembered over the dinner at Sundial, Kristiaan promised my dad he would take the stress for both of us so I could pursue whatever my heart desires. Kristiaan touched me with his love, which sometimes meant taking on the strain for two so I could have time and space all to myself.

"I love you *more*! I'm just happy to see you enjoy your time. That's more than enough to make my day," he said with an endearing smile. "I will make up our Valentine's for you when you come back. I can't wait for you to be back in just a few more days."

The next few days flew by. I tried many more things for the first time. At Long Bay, I rode a horse along the beach, and it cantered into the ocean like a high-powered motorboat. Waves splashed onto my lap and propelled us forward. I also squeezed in a day trip to Grand Turks, where I saw a swarm of wild flamingos bask in the sun and then fly away all at the same time, like flames in the air.

By the end of my stay at Turks and Caicos, I had made many indelible memories. However, none of them had my family and boyfriend in them. They were the reason I felt safe and motivated enough to travel solo in the first place. But I now missed their presence immensely.

I craved to return to Kristiaan, to my home.

But first, one more detour.

CHAPTER 30

Island Hopping

———

I felt the mild ocean breeze as I boarded the Celebrity Silhouette cruise ship on a late Sunday afternoon. My heart told me that Kristiaan could wait, but a few more days on the islands could not. I needed more time to be alone before I returned to real life, filled with challenges and uncertainties.

After a couple of crisp and loud honks, the cruise ship departed from the port. My voyage to more tropical islands started. One of my traveling habits was to familiarize myself with my surroundings on the first day of my trip. I preferred to explore all the opportunities to have options to choose from. I brought my phone and left my room to walk around the ship.

Bars and restaurants were clustered on the third and fifth decks. Swirl pools and hot tubs were scattered across the twelfth deck. Many early birds had already dipped into the pool to relax in the water. A spa was located near the front of the ship. Looking down from above, I could see a dance floor with an ivory grand piano on the side at the grand foyer.

Convenience and luxury were at my fingertips. Everything was well-prepared and exquisitely designed. I knew my cruise experience would starkly contrast with my solo traveling experience in the past two-and-a-half weeks. I didn't need to worry about anything—where to have dinner, how to navigate around, or what I could do at my destinations. However, convenience took away the thrill—everything was too predictable to be fun, and deep in the unknown often lay the treasure of a rewarding adventure. I thought cruising was a great way to get a taste of multiple places, and then I could decide where to stay for an extended amount of time for my next vacation.

The only thing troubling me was after I returned home, I still would have no idea what to do with my life. My hectic graduate school experience pushed me to a dead end, and I was completely burnt out. While on vacation, with all the time in the world to think and wonder, I wanted to dive into the things that would make me wake up excited every day.

The problem was, I had no clue what that was. Hopefully, I'd have some ideas by the end of my island-hopping.

During days at sea, my time was spent working out at the gym, attending art auctions, reading, and taking a soak in the hot tub. Just around sunset, I went to the top deck and watched the sky painted in candy colors. I knew the sunset could usually inspire a great idea or two. In case some great ideas sparked, I often watched the sunset with a journal in hand so I could jot them down instantly while they were hot and fresh.

When I watched the sun get closer to the horizon and the sea shimmer with the gold flare of the sun, a few thoughts popped into my head. I was thinking without the distractions of my day-to-day tasks or any school or relationship pressures to make me anxious.

The question came back to me: What do I want to do with my life so I can feel fulfilled and happy?

I noticed that, when free from expectations or deadlines, I longed to reconnect with my passions in the arts and express myself as a storyteller. So I immediately wrote those ideas down in my notebook. Reflecting on my past few years and my solo traveling experience, I realized events in life would never be constant, and the only constant in life was change. Occasionally, the inability to welcome change was disruptive. Stress, anxiety, fear, and sadness would find their way back to me. If I could define the endeavors I would love to pour my life into, then I would have the boundless energy to overcome those negative mindsets and find strength in trying times.

Those thoughts were clues. I did not have a complete answer yet, but those clues were a start. Besides, I had a whole journey to ponder my answers.

Our first stop was St. Croix. While most of the cruise guests chose to be beach bums, I went to be an apprentice at an art studio for a day and learn woodcraft. It was my first time carving a raw piece of log into a piece of wood art. Never did I realize the amount of effort and creativity put into those wood crafts until I spent four-and-a-half hours making a vase. I started by cutting the log and rolling it on a wood lathe until the rough sides were smooth and shiny. And then I started to mold the wood into the shape of a vase with a slim neck and chubby belly. Applying beeswax onto the surface made the wood look earthy and rich. Then I used a knife to carve out the design I wanted—a flamingo.

My wood vase was taking form in my hand as I approached the end polish. By the end of the woodworking session, I felt a deep sense of achievement.

During those four-and-a-half hours, my inner artist came to life. My bliss made me oblivious to the burning sensation from the splinters that cut through my skin while I polished my wood vase on the wood lathe. I thought the magic of passion was that it could make me forget any distractions and just focus on my craft. Learning the art of woodcraft helped me find one piece of the puzzle of pursuing my passion—it took persistence and devotion to build my own successful project. Though the process might not be glamorous, the sense of achievement and the excitement of starting something from scratch were well worth my effort.

The next day, our ship docked at Antigua. My day started with swimming with stingrays at a private lagoon. When I fed them with squids, I got to feel their coconut jelly skin with my fingers. Sometimes, a couple of sneaky sting rays touched my legs while they were swimming around. Their skin was so silky, so when I had an up-close and personal encounter with the stingrays, I felt as if I was having a spa. After I jumped out of the water, I went horseback riding around the island. When I reached the top of a mountain, the sweeping view of the island and the topaz Caribbean water was beneath me. It was so picturesque that it looked more artistic than a landscape painting.

As I indulged myself in my unique first-time experiences, I became more motivated to continue seeking new ventures. The bold spirit I inherited from my dad was rekindled by my therapeutic voyage. I knew when the infliction from my past no longer held me back, I could embrace the present and live each day to the fullest. Proactively trying new things restored my power to create my own happiness and prepared me for the hardships and gifts in the future. After healing myself from the trauma, I believed I had become a stronger person, so I dove into my next challenge.

At my third destination, St. Lucia, I felt particularly ambitious, so I decided to climb Gros Piton, which is 2,619 feet (798 meters) high.[7] The hike was strenuous not only because of the rocky and steep path on the way up but also because of the scorching heat that made me feel exhausted soon after I began. When I reached the mid-way point, my legs felt soft like jelly and my breath became heavier. My body was soaked with sweat. When I looked up, more precarious-looking rocks blocked the path, at which point my guide said we needed to rock climb. Then I looked down and saw that the cliff led straight into the water. I had no choice but to keep climbing. I thought midpoint was the most challenging position. It would be a shame to go back down the same way I climbed up, given how much rocky path I had already overcome. There was still much to climb, and it would only get more difficult.

When we reached the final quarter of our hike, my body started collapsing every step I took upward. I was panting heavily and felt lightheaded. My limbs were droopy, and my fear mounted because if I lost my attention any second, one misstep could result in me rolling down the hill into the abyss. "Are you sure you want to continue?" My guide asked me.

At first, I was adamant about making it to the top, especially because of how much closer I was. Because of the time constraint and my body sending me signals of my physical limits, I grudgingly sat down on a rock to take a break.

7   "Hiking St. Lucia Pitons," Islander Villa Escapes, accessed October 6, 2020.

"You know, sometimes it is also wise to know when to quit. Listen to your body. Don't try to force it, especially since you have to save your energy for downhill too." My guide tried to console me.

After the break, we headed down to the ship. I could not help but relate climbing Gros Piton to my graduate school experience. Though I quit the master's program, I learned I needed to listen to my heart and my body. If I felt exhausted and burned out every day, it was time to pause and consider whether I needed to switch to a different path.

My time in Barbados and Grenada was relaxing and low-key. I explored a few rain forests where I discovered many vibrant-colored tropical flowers. I also got the opportunity to lure some wild green monkeys to eat bananas on my head. I felt in sync with nature, and it brought me so much joy to lose myself on the island.

The last destination of my island-hopping was St. Kitts. I wanted to conclude my voyage with a high note, so I found myself on the top of a mountain, about to glide down to the ground through a zip line. In fact, I did three courses, and each of them was known for speed, height, or both. After the thrill, I decided to unwind by doing a painting at a historic estate. A table and art supplies were set up under a giant palm tree. I wanted to create a piece of art that I could take home to always remind me of my island adventures. So I decided to paint a green monkey, the one that peeled bananas on my head.

"You should be proud, Ms. Yuan! There were only three people signed up to climb Gros Pitons, and you were the only one bringing back a painting done by yourself," the excursions manager said when I returned to my cruise ship.

"Wow, this makes me feel so special." I was elated by his compliments.

"You *are* special. Hope you enjoy the rest of the cruise," the manager said.

I promised to keep saying this to myself whenever I was in doubt—I *am* special.

During the sea days before we docked at Fort Lauder-dale, I revisited the question I asked myself at the start of this cruise. It became ever more apparent to me that before I did anything else, I needed to write this book. The power of telling my stories lies in helping me track my growth. Even more importantly, it lies in helping others to hopefully embark on their own adventures. I wanted to combine my passion for traveling, storytelling, and creating art along the way. It brought me so much sense of achievement to explore the beauty of landscapes and locals during my solo travels and would bring me more felicity if I could make the world a bit more stunning.

Finding my true calling was the ultimate gift I received from my time on the islands. The compass would guide me through my next steps.

CHAPTER 31

Crazy Love

———

After a month of hopping from island to island in the Caribbean, I finally landed my feet on the ground again. My luggage was filled with treasures I collected or created on the islands—conch shells, a sea fan, a painting of a Mona green monkey, a straw bag, and some rum cakes.

But the most important treasure I brought back was a new sense of direction.

My resolve to stick with the endeavors that energized me became ever more clear. Though I did not know the specific role I would play in the world, it would combine traveling, storytelling, and art-making. And my first step was to write a book about how I reached this eureka moment.

After my flight landed in Atlanta, the crowds at the airport and the chilly weather woke me up to the real world. I felt like I'd fallen from cloud nine. Little did I know that after passing customs, I'd be sent to secondary inspection by a staff member. Without any explanation, the person led me into a room with glass walls. The room was dead silent, and everyone in the room looked depressed and anxious. It felt like a goldfish bowl without water, and the people waiting inside looked like dying fish.

A surge of fear loomed over my head. *What would happen now? Never had I been sent to secondary inspection, so what is wrong this time?* No one was making eye contact with each other or making any sound. On the glass wall, a big poster said, "Report to an officer for sexual assault..."

My anxiety rose up to my throat when I saw those words.

Hey, I don't know why but I am in secondary inspection. Don't know when I can get out of here, I quickly texted Kristiaan.

Calm down, sweetheart. I am not going anywhere until I see you. I'm here for you. He was waiting outside of the airport at the pickup area already.

It's so scary. There's this poster on the wall about sexual assault... No one is speaking a word. And I don't know what will happen, I followed up.

I will break into that place if I have to. I won't allow anyone to lay a finger on you. Try to keep calm. It's a stress test. Kristiaan kept reminding me to keep my cool.

The clock was ticking, and no one knew what would happen. The worst kind of psychological stress was deadly silence, and not knowing when it would ever come to an end. To distract myself from the crazy thoughts about how things could go wrong, I took out my journal book and tried to calm myself down by reading about my island adventures.

A lady who looked like she was in her late twenties sat next to me. She looked at my journal a few times and finally said, "You are a great writer!"

"Oh, thanks!" I was happy about her compliment. It was probably the only thing that felt humane and warm in the cold goldfish bowl.

Soon we began to make small talk to kill time. It had been two hours since I first stepped into the waiting room.

"So how long have you been waiting?" I asked her.

"Three hours now. There are folks here who have been waiting for five hours and still haven't gotten any replies," she whispered in a heavy tone.

"Wow. Is it so bad that now I feel a little bit more composed after hearing what you just said?" I tried to be sarcastic and release some of my fears and anxiety.

"Haha, you are funny. But you are right, it could be much worse. What's your name?" She chuckled quietly.

"Mary. You?" I asked back.

"Ella," she said.

"I flew in from Romania and was planning to visit my friends for the weekend here in Atlanta. Every time, there was no problem. Who knows what is wrong this time? I even thought earlier it had something to do with COVID-19," Ella explained further.

"It's likely..." I ran out of words to say because my emotions were still churning in my stomach. Ella reminded me that there was a pandemic exploding around the world. On March 6, there'd been no outbreak in the US yet, but everywhere else in the world, especially in China, where I am from, it had been months of shutdown, and many deaths.

My worries piled up, and I could not imagine what I would do if I needed to immediately book the next flight to

Beijing. The thought of not being able to return to Kristiaan consumed me and intensified my fear.

What if I could not say goodbye to Kristiaan before I flew home in a hurry? What would this separation from him mean? Questions mushroomed in my head. Though these were merely my worries, they could very well be a reality at any second. The thought of how drastically things could turn upside down reminded me of the unforeseeable nature of life once again. Just as I could not predict my parents' divorce, the external factors beyond my control would affect my relationship with Kristiaan. It became more vital not to forget the significance of cherishing the present because I never knew what would happen next.

At that moment, my conflicts with Kristiaan no longer bothered me as much as the possibility that we might not see each other again. I yearned to hold him tightly and share with him the lessons I had learned during my travels. *Please don't make it worse and let me get back to Kristiaan.* The last time I prayed was when I sat by my dad's bed in his quarantine room at the hospital.

I tried to think about Kristiaan's text—"try to calm down"—and the positive mentality I brought with me from the island. *Everything is going to be alright,* I kept telling myself.

A few minutes later, someone called my name. I met with a female officer and answered a few questions about where I had been in the past couple of months. Then I was released, just like that. The fear and anxiety that had been choking me suddenly collapsed and vanished into thin air.

I escaped from the goldfish bowl like a fish leaping into the ocean, free and happy. When I saw Kristiaan at the arrival level, he ran toward me and lifted me from the ground.

"I was worried sick. I was almost going to break into the room and speak with whoever I needed to speak with. I was so worried anything bad would happen to you. And then I would never be able to forgive myself." Kristiaan then held me close in his arms.

"I could not believe what just happened either. I mean, at one point, I literally said, 'Over the past month traveling solo in the Caribbean islands, I was just trying to figure out my shit.' And the officer laughed so hard." I shared with Kristiaan the absurd roller coaster of intense emotions that had consumed me in the past three hours.

"I bet your humor helped you get out faster. I am just happy you are finally here. I missed you so much." Kristiaan then said he had been waiting in the car the entire time and his body was shaking, yet he tried to tell me to calm down.

He took me to his car, and we escaped from the airport in seconds. It was already 10:00 p.m., and there was no traffic that late in Atlanta. So Kristiaan sped down the highway.

"I am so happy that you are home!" he said again and again.

"Same. I've thought a lot this past month and I was ready to be back," I said.

Then Kristiaan started kissing me vigorously, while still trying to keep his eyes on the road. He kept doing that and I tried to pull him away and told him to be careful, yet he nodded and kept kissing. After twenty minutes, I realized we were still not home yet, so I knew he had just been driving to nowhere.

"Do you know where we are?" I stole a moment to ask him.

"Don't care! It's not that big of a city. We'll find our way back." Kristiaan kept kissing my lips, cheeks, and my neck.

I felt a flame of passion in my heart as Kristiaan showered me with his kisses. "You know you are crazy, right?" I said.

"Crazily in love with you, yes. And you are crazy too." He seemed bothered by my many questions.

While I lost myself in his burning love, I realized the crisis I handled earlier brought Kristiaan and I even closer. The thought that we might never see each other again, or the possibility that I might have had to book a flight back home, made us both realize how unpredictable things could be, and neither of us could know what would happen next.

When I was back in Kristiaan's arms, I knew I was finally home after over a month of soul-searching and solo traveling. There was nothing else for me to worry about. I could fully enjoy the moment of reunion, the warm and heartfelt moment of being home with Kristiaan.

PART 6

REBUILDING MY HOME

"What I tried to find across the globe on
my own had, in fact, been there with me
the whole time."

CHAPTER 32

Home Amid COVID-19

Only a few days after I returned to Atlanta from my month-long island adventures, COVID-19 exploded across the US. The number of infections and death toll started surging from the hundreds to the tens of thousands. States like New York were under a shutdown. Social distancing was being practiced nationwide. Restaurants only offered curbside pickup. People rushed into the grocery stores to hoard toilet paper. Companies demanded their employees work from home until further notice. Suddenly, the world was thrown into the new normal in a mere couple of weeks. The uncertainty of what would happen next kept people awake at night and aroused more fear and sadness when they awoke to bad news every morning.

The world slowed down during the pandemic, as everyone was following the "shelter-in-place" recommendation from government officials. The economy plummeted. Flights were canceled. Some cruises were stranded in the oceans where passengers were infected without knowing when they could disembark. Travelers were stuck in hotels without a means to go back home. Graduations for the Class of 2020 got canceled or postponed. In a flurry of instructions and orders, people quickly refocused on the essentials—staying home with family more than ever, sanitizing the living space more frequently and thoroughly, and prioritizing connections over work by hopping on Zoom meetings to show care and love.

COVID-19 also accelerated the trends already underway. Remote working became a novel concept that the workforce had to adapt to rapidly. Many unilateral relationships started decoupling because of heated political tensions and finger-pointing accusations amid a global pandemic. Deglobalization was a word that had been buzzing for a while yet felt ever more imminent. Without in-person lecturing, higher education had to reconsider how to justify its value in light of the soaring price tag of tuition.

The moment Kristiaan drove me back to his place from the airport, it felt as if I'd been living in another world this past month, unaware of the dangerously severe and intense world in which everyone else was living.

Kristiaan had prepared many items to brace for the upcoming peaks of the pandemic. He bought bags of N95 and M100 masks before the rising cases emerged in Atlanta. Under our bed, there were multiple containers of Clorox wipes, bottles of hand sanitizer, hand soap, and gloves.

"You know, you are *so* lucky. You literally crossed the line between normalcy and outbreak. Had you chosen to come back a couple of days later, I don't think you would have even been able to come back," Kristiaan said.

"I know. I feel that way too. I would have been stranded in the Caribbean if I returned just one or two days later. I know that a couple of passengers were sick on the cruise and flight right after mine," I said.

Vidur, a photographer who worked on the cruise ship and created a photo album for me, told me about the worrisome outbreak on the cruise ship through a WhatsApp message.

I could not imagine what I would do if I was stranded, away from Kristiaan, without any family members around. We both felt relieved I was back in one piece, and we would quarantine together amid this global pandemic.

Kristiaan moved his office stuff to our bedroom and started working from home. With a laptop and a vigorous brain, I started creating this book. There was no better time for me to write than now, given all the time I had on my hands. I could finally buckle down to ruminate my key take-aways from my experiences over the past few years without any distractions or deadlines.

Meanwhile, to add a little color to my life, I kept growing two pots of garden roses to watch them flourish from buds to luscious blossoms. It was a promising sign of growth in a world battling death.

My sense of creativity and acute desire to write became more salient. During this critical time, although I was not one of the medics battling COVID-19 on the frontline, I chose to do my part by staying at home to write my stories and connect with others in a meaningful way.

As a first-time author, I gathered my motivation from my purpose to connect people and hopefully inspire them through this uncertain and turbulent time. If I could bring a thread of sunshine into people's lives through my book, then I would have done something beautiful in this world.

I have always believed that the power of stories lies in the genuine connections people could build, regardless of their backgrounds. Through my writing, I hoped to bring people together during this divided time.

My idea of bringing people together started with inviting my audience to contemplate the meaning of home.

Where is home? And what is home?

Home for me, during COVID-19, was connecting with my family and trying to cheer each other on to power through this challenging time. Though I was physically away from my family, we were brought closer together by our weekly video calls. I video chatted with Mom, Grandma, and Dad every week to check in with them and make sure they were healthy and well.

"Hey, Mom and Grandma, how are things going in Beijing?" I asked in Mandarin when I called home.

"The containment is very strict here. We are actually more worried about YOU! We've heard the cases in the US spiraled out of control." Mom looked concerned.

"It is, but Kristiaan and I are staying at home. We are not going anywhere except getting groceries occasionally. And don't worry, we wear masks, wash hands, and take a shower right after we step indoors again." I reassured Mom that Kristiaan and I were practicing social distancing and sanitization.

"Call us every week so that we get a timely update from you. Or else we are always worried sick about you," Grandma insisted.

Then I would call Dad separately, and we mostly talked about my career plans. He wanted me to have a clear sense of direction even in a time of confusion and uncertainty.

"I'm so proud of you for writing a book! I've always believed that you should stick to what you love. Remember how you liked expressing yourself through singing, dancing, and painting as a kid? I think now you continue sharing your stories with the world through your writing." Dad looked elated when he talked about my book journey.

"Thanks, Dad! How are your projects going?" Getting approval from my dad was not usually easy, so I felt particularly exhilarated.

"We are planning a few upcoming exhibitions virtually and have several projects already lined up after the shutdown." He seemed to be satisfied with the rebound of his art business. I knew he could do it.

My love for my family grew more intense during this time of crisis. My conflicting feelings regarding my relationship with my dad since my parents' divorce no longer existed. I only cared that everyone in my family was safe. Dad mailed me more masks and some medicine in case of emergency. The package did not arrive until two months later, but his love for me was not delayed one bit.

My home was also the place I shared with Kristiaan. We had been through the crisis of our relationship, and now a global pandemic, but the love between us grew as a result. Regardless of Kristiaan's betrayal, he had been trying every single waking moment to hopefully win my trust back. And now, he was the only person who could take care of me to make sure I was safe and healthy. He has been doing the job of my parents when they could not physically be here with me.

In a way, COVID-19 helped highlight the important things in life. Every day, I reexamine my priorities, and it turns out that the people who love me and the ones I love come on top of everything else. Many of my friends also intentionally spend more time with their families by cooking for their parents or having a movie night with their siblings. We also realize that during a pandemic, checking on friends and families becomes a priority. It can be awkward sometimes given long period of disconnection, but we are so excited to see our old friends, whom we have known since primary school. It only takes a text on Messenger to hop on a Zoom chat.

I believe home becomes especially precious to us when we navigate through unpredictable times. It provides us with security and stability regardless of the chaos outside. I have found while searching across the globe that home is what I create with the people I love and those who care for me. Home is no longer constrained to a physical location, and it is essentially where I am with the special people in my life. I think somewhere deep down, my power to forgive helped me out of my years of misery, endowed me with the capacity to give Dad and Kristiaan a second chance, and also strengthened the home I rebuilt.

CHAPTER 33

Where Is Home?

———

In the past few years, I had traveled the world to find home.

The home I used to know, the one that was complete, no longer existed. Home used to mean where my family was, especially where my parents were together. When it was no longer an option for me, I tried to build a new home with my own hands.

My journey of rebuilding home has opened my eyes to the possibilities of what home could be. Now that I have solo traveled to Dubai, Italy, France, Israel, Switzerland, and the Caribbean, I would say home is what you make it.

Home lives through the connections I built with total strangers, who were generous and kind enough to make a totally foreign place warm and inviting. Their love for their own families and the hospitality they showed me reminded me of my own family. So I stopped running away from my own family and chose to reconnect with them. I tried to bring together the broken pieces and build a new home.

However, it was not the major way for me to regain my sense of belonging. To truly resolve the afflictions of the past that had been torturing me, I needed to face my new reality, and it started with repairing the relationship between my dad and I.

He video called me the other day to check in on me. He sensed he had lost my unconditional trust in him, so he said, "瑶瑶，别对你爸这么没信心哈。(Yaoyao, don't have so little faith in me.)"

I knew that was his way of saying, "I will try my best to make you feel that you can depend on me like before." He also talked about reviving his art gallery business. Dad looked exceptionally optimistic when he shared with me that he secured a few promising projects that would bring back the glory to his palace. Whether or not those projects could truly help Dad achieve an astounding comeback was not important to me. What mattered was his confidence and resolve, and I was so delighted that he was in good spirits again. The dad I had been missing returned.

I attribute the improvement of my relationship with my dad to what my mom said at the boutique suit shop in Amsterdam: "What happened between your dad and I should not interfere with your attitude toward him." Whenever I have conflicting feelings for Dad again, my mom's reminder replays in my head.

My mom and I have become even closer after going through our healing processes together. After hearing about her love stories and her reasons to stick with Dad when I was younger, I appreciate more of the sacrifices she made to give me a merry childhood.

"妈妈只能给你这么多，接下来的路你要自己学着走啦。(Mom can only give you so much. You have to learn how to live your life,)" she said, encouraging me to be an independent grown-up during a recent video chat.

She also told me repeatedly how proud she was of my decision to publish my story and hopefully uplift people around the world. During the days when I doubted myself, Mom would say, "世上只有一个袁梦瑶。你要相信自己的独特之处还有无限的正能量。(The world has only one Yaoyao. You have to believe in your uniqueness and your limitless positivity to create an impact.)" Mom is my compass when I lose my way and need to rediscover my sense of direction. I also find our similar current love stories divinely connected—knowing she has someone now by her side to pamper her ardently makes me satisfied; and she feels the same about my relationship with Kristiaan.

Mom was absolutely right—we cannot let one person destroy our capacity to love. Betrayal can happen, but what the person chooses to do to rebuild the trust is what counts. Without my mom's advice, I don't think I would have given Kristiaan a second chance, and we would not be a loving couple powering through the global pandemic together like a family.

I also called Grandma recently to tell her how excited I am to visit her again after the pandemic. The glow in her eyes when she saw me, even if just on the screen, conveyed how tremendously she adores me. She is always the one in my family who tirelessly asks me to prioritize my health. Even though they were simple things like drinking more water, eating fresh fruits daily, or sleeping for at least eight hours a night, Grandma's detailed reminders showed her delicate love for me. When I asked her about her health, she told me not to worry and gave me a thumbs-up with her iconic radiant smile. At the end of each of our video calls, Grandma would say, "要和大金毛儿好好的。(You and Kristiaan should be good.)" She hopes my relationship with Kristiaan can grow stronger and that I am happy and loved.

As for Kristiaan, he often reminds me that he is part of my family. Time and his genuine effort to regain my trust helped him save our near-death relationship. Sporadically, I tease him about how his mistakes can never be forgiven, but he just says, "I will try harder so that you can hopefully love me again."

Reflecting upon the bonds I share with Mom, Dad, Grandma, and Kristiaan, I realize they might not always be as flawless as I thought they were. However, I no longer want a perfect family because they are *my* family. It is a blessing to be loved by every one of them, and that's everything I need.

What I tried to find across the globe on my own had, in fact, been there with me the whole time. It took time for me to see what was right in front of me. I feel so relieved and blessed that the unresolved pain that haunted me is now replaced by the affection my family has for me. I recalled what my mom loves to say when she cooks noodles: "Every good dish starts with a solid base." I believe the foundation that was once broken is finally restored, so I no longer feel uprooted and lost, but grounded at home.

The best part is that in addition to rebuilding my sense of home, I also have gained the capacity to embrace whatever life throws at me. The fear I had before cannot weigh me down anymore. I know that even if I get lost again, I am resilient enough to find my way back. If life throws another challenge at me, I might not know how to cope right away, but I know I will not forget the positive attitude I planted in my heart while I was island hopping.

To those also navigating through the turbulent feelings of betrayal by family, friends, or loved ones, *you* hold the power of healing. The answers to your questions about life are within you. The first step to finding those answers is to start living and accepting the present. Embark on your own adventures. Losing yourself in your travels will bring you closer to rediscovering your identity. It is absolutely necessary to take your time. Do not rush the process.

Though I thought I was solo traveling to find home, in fact, the support from the people who loved me had empowered me every step of the way. I hoped everything would get better with my efforts to rebuild my home. My dad and Kristiaan made their mistakes and broke my trust in them; however, I learned to give them a second chance to love me. The ups and downs of my relationships with my family made me realize that people might not be what I thought them to be, but their love for me fueled their determination to act upon their mistakes and try to make things right.

Now I am finishing up this book, with Kristiaan cooking me dinner and taking me out over the weekend for a hike among the mountains with no one else around. Looking around, I see roses blooming, and the person who loves me supporting me since the start of my writing process. I can see the home I rebuilt start to blossom as well. I feel more anchored than ever.

I hope my stories entice you to embark on your own adventures and explore where home is for you. To aspiring solo travelers out there, I hope my solo traveling experience motivates you to take the first step toward your dream destinations by booking your next flight. I also implore you to consider rebuilding the broken trust you share with your loved ones.

As you try finding your definition of home, remember that home is more than a physical location. It can be the people who love and care for you, or even complete strangers who want to make you feel at home. Home can be wherever you are, or an evolving space that you create. My stories have shown you the numerous possibilities of what home can be. The secret is that finding home is a dynamic process, and as you go through more experiences, the definitions develop accordingly.

I have shared with you my expedition of finding home, and I hope you got to know me better. Now it's time for you to delve into the meaning of home and look for your own answers.

Hundreds of pages later, ask yourself again—where is home?

***

I hope love and gratitude will be passed along with my memoir. Whichever way we would like to define home; it is a place where we feel the most in sync with ourselves. My wish is that my book can inspire more heartening conversations about home and our identities so people can feel closer to each other despite the divisive time we live in.

Nothing can bring me more joy and fulfillment as an author than knowing my stories can lighten up the world, one soul at a time.

ACKNOWLEDGMENTS

My memoir was written, edited, and published during a global pandemic. The year 2020 is a special year not only filled with uncertainties and grief, but also immense strength and breakthroughs. It is a blessing to seize the opportunity to pursue my dream during this unprecedented time of crisis. Although I am not one of the medics battling against the virus on the frontline, my choice to do my part is staying at home as a fierce writer hoping to empower others with my stories. Thank you, 2020, for pushing me to grow.

This heartfelt, uplifting, and magical book journey would not be possible without the unconditional love and strong faith of my family, who is on the other side of the world. Mom, thanks for showing me the power of love and strength in vulnerability. Grandma, thanks for always reminding me of my uniqueness, potential, and my resilience whenever I am in doubt. Dad, this is hard for me to say given our complicated relationship since the divorce, but thanks for endowing me with the independent spirit to travel the world alone without fear.

During tough days when my creative juices ran out, Honey and Dots, my Alaskan malamute and hybrid, who have been growing with me for eight years, never ceased to put a smile on my face. Despite the challenges my family has been through, thanks, Mom and Grandma, for raising me to become a strong person with character, values, and a deep sense of home and belonging.

Kristiaan, although you broke my heart once, and our relationship almost did not survive, I appreciate that you have been trying harder each day to make me feel at home away from home. Thanks to you, I have a place across the Pacific where I feel I belong. My mom and I are grateful that you can be by my side when my family can't, and that our relationship turned out to be pandemic-proof.

Professor Christine Ristaino, you are the first person who discovered the sbalorditivo (stunning) and potent voice in my storytelling. If it was not for your profound mentorship and belief in me from the day I enrolled in your memoir class three years ago, I would never have imagined that one day I would become a published author. Thanks for always seeing the unique glow in my persona and appreciating my beautiful soul.

Celia, you know I would not be writing in English today without your teaching since I was in primary school. I am grateful that when the publishing campaign was slow, you helped me pass the finish line and freed me from anxiety and stress. Also, thank you for helping my mom power through her difficult time when I could not physically be there.

Professor Eric Koester, who knew our first LinkedIn message and fifteen-minute chat would blossom into my transformative publishing journey? Your devotion to creativity and passion is beyond commendable, and I am lucky that you recognized the potential and impact of my stories. Thanks for cheering me on as I reach for the stars.

Rajiv, I deeply appreciate your encouragement since day one of my book journey. I'm thankful that we connected through LinkedIn, and that you are willing to listen to my wild startup ideas and offer guidance. Michael, you are the best commenter and editor I know. Thanks for offering detailed and helpful feedback for my manuscript.

Yupeng Lu, Jingyu Zhang, Wenyi Xu, Ziran Li, Jianglai Zhang, Yana, Kiran, Michelle, Asma, Emma, and Eboni, I am lucky to have you as my long-time amazing friends. I am grateful to have known you as far back as eight years ago.

Brian Bies, you said, "It takes a village to publish a book." Absolutely, so I want to show my gratitude to the dream publishing team at New Degree Press. I've learned so much about engaging with an audience, building my brand, and amplifying my voice this year. It's much more than publishing my first book. Brian Bies, Haley Newlin, MacKenzie Finklea, Kyra Ann Dawkins, Leila Summers, Heather Gomez, Lyn Solares, and Jamie Tibasco. Thank you.

"Good books are written, but *great* books are edited," Brian pointed out in one of the weekly authors' workshops. Special thanks to Elina Oliferovskiy, Karina Agbisit, Kristy Elam, and Venus Bradley. Thanks for loving my shitty first draft as much as I did and helping me turn it into gold. Elina, you were a phenomenal coach in helping me with marketing strategies. I saw my prose and writing improve every day with your detailed feedback and edits. Thank you for pouring hours of effort into helping me polish my craft.

***

My dream of publishing my memoir would not be possible without the tremendous love and support of my 149 early proud backers from seventeen countries and six continents. Thank you for your vote of confidence in me as a debut author, backing my book campaign, and purchasing my memoir long before publication. You are my champions who are the first to see the exceptional potential, timely relevance, and empowering significance of my stories. I am lucky to have shared my publishing journey with all of you from the beginning. The magic of my four-leaf clovers worked! Thank you all:

Special thanks

Xianqin Meng, Hong Zhang, Qiulai Yuan, Kristiaan Sheedy, Rajiv Kapoor, Celia Tian, Robynne Bruckenstein, Laura Garcia, Matt Staebell, Frances Thomas, Michael Chang, James Wang, Harry Lu, Luis M Guillen, Andrew Haines, Iris Hoskins, Richard E. Brodsky, Maggie and Tom Sheedy, Melissa Sheedy, Kevin Zhen, Eric Li, Max Pitaksit, Shivam Agarwal, Jane Jingyu Zhang, Ling Sun, Lijo Mathew, Hannah Smith.

I also appreciate

Leslie Mariscal, Ravi Kiran Goli, Athena Richardson, Kevin Liang, Shannon Case, Leor Elfassy, Wenyi Xu, Pauline Madriz, Jennifer Radke, Zachary Prell, Jordan McKenna, Marianne Hynd, Erin Schwartz, Samantha Tall, Katherine Hochrein, Dr. Hayley Vatcher, Anastacia M Valdespino, Agasha Ratam, Wendy Zhan, Qiulai Yuan, Jianglai Zhang, Chidi Onwuka, Denee Headen, Shirley Ye, Katie Woolard, Abbas Raza, Priyanka Surio, Weiyi Gong, Alyssa Banguilan, Keagan Sacripanti, Carmen Delehanty, Elizabeth Hicks,

Rania Svoronou, Yang Li, Yun-Te Sung, David Gregoire, Alice Oh, Maximilian Adlerstraahle, Ana Galvez, Romina Damini, Rachel Tao, Ryan Yuan Lee, Fiona von Grey, Jennifer Nau, Eric Koester, Charlene Wang, Daisy Bugarin, Hannah Mosleym Cher Hu, Michael Kotarinos, Katherine Sheedy, Christine Ristaino, Dasani Madipalli, Jane Jingyu Zhang, Belinda Lei, Danny Weeks, Bowei Oki, Derek Buffardi, Saurabh Parimal Doodhwala, Duanchen Liu, Dezmon Scott, Aditya Patwardhan, Shanmukha Srivathsav Satujoda, Livi Redden, Katie Cassedy, Emma Jost-Price, Ayana Dickens, Olivia Fogel, Oscar Escobar, Cady North, Debbie Stone, Rachel Curl, Esther Ray, Joquinn Thomas Sadler, Raymond W. Curl, Judy McCormick, Wenbin Gao, Alex Mckenzie, Ansley Sheedy, Matthew Wilkerson, Tiffany Mosher, Sophia Nemeth, Kiran S. Sundar, Robert Gotwals, Leo Xu, Rachel Curl, Ted Willis, Russel Abad, Jina Park, Johanna Lund, Vidur Suddul, Alice Qiu, Thamina Stoll, Margaret Mckenzie, Jonathan Osei, Bethany Larson, Brianna Karpowich, Brandon Karpowich, Dylan Frank, Hatty Wang, Honoka Nakamachi, Patricia Martes, Puppy Cai, Danielle Hughes, Dan Sheedy, Margot Bailowitz, Anusha Gadipudi, Eboni Freeman, Ashley Boren, Asma Syed, Hayoung Roh, Alli Esker, Ashok Bhatraju, Michelle Zhao, Mary Grace Stoneking, Bevan Penn, Francis Wilson, Prince Sewani, and Anna Cheniuntai.

GLOSSARY (MANDARIN)

EXPRESSIONS

倍儿香!

Bei-er Xiang! (Yummy!)

吃糖太多容易有蛀牙。

Chi Tang Taiduo Yongyi You Zhuya. (Eating too many candies can cause cavities.)

感激当下。

Ganji Dangxia. (Appreciate the moment.)

很高兴见到您!

Hen Gao Xing Jiandao Nin. (So glad to meet you!)

麻将

Ma Jiang (Mahjong)

你好!

Ni Hao! (Hello!)

你叫什么名字?

Ni Jiao Shenme Mingzi? (What's your name?)

年

Nian (Year; also refers to the symbol of bad luck, which is a monster who haunts families at the year's end, according to Chinese folklore)

生日快乐!

Shengri Kuaile! (Happy birthday!)

体力可不如以前了!

Tili Buru Yiqian Le! (My stamina is not as strong as before.)

提前祝您母亲节快乐!

Tiqian Zhu Nin Muqin Jie Kuaile! (Happy Mother's Day in advance!)

五子棋

Wu Zi Qi (Gomoku)

我想死你啦。

Wo Xiang Si Ni La. (I miss you so much.)

想吃点儿什么?

Xiang Chi Dian-er Shenme? (What do you want to eat?)

在一起的感觉真好。

Zai Yiqi De Ganjue Zhenhao. (It feels so good to be together.)

这景色太美啦!

Zhe Jingse Taimei La! (The view is stunning!)

这是我的男朋友。

Zhe Shi Wode Nan Pengyou. (This is my boyfriend.)

FOOD

艾窝窝	*Ai Wo Wo* (One of my favorite traditional snacks in Beijing, made of sticky rice and red bean sauce)
长寿面	*Chang Shou Mian* (Long-life Noodles, and my mom makes the most delicious ones)
豆腐脑	*Dou Fu Nao* (Tofu stew, my grandma's favorite traditional breakfast food in Beijing)
豆浆	*Dou Jiang* (Soymilk)
饺子	*Jiao Zi* (Chinese dumplings, and my grandma makes the best ones)
糖油饼	*Tang You Bing* (Fried sugar dough, another traditional breakfast food in Beijing)

IDIOMS AND WORDS OF WISDOM

好聚好散。	*Hao Ju Hao San.* (Meet and part on good terms.)
家和万事兴。	*Jia He Wan Shi Xing.* (Everything in life prospers when the family is in harmony.)
家家有本儿难念的经。	*Jia Jia You Ben-er Nan Nian De Jing.* (Every family has gone through difficulties unknown by the public.)
解铃还需系铃人。	*Jie Ling Hai Xu Ji Ling Ren.* ("Only the person who tied a bell on the tiger's neck can untie the bell." It implies a problem can only be solved by whoever caused it.)
善行无辙迹, 善言无瑕谪。	*Shan Xing Wu Zhe Ji, Shan Yan Wu Xia Zhe.* (A famous quote by the renowned ancient Chinese philosopher Lao Tzu, but not a literal English translation—a good traveler has no fixed plans and is not intent on arriving.)
身体是革命的本钱!	*Shenti Shi Geming De Benqian.* (Health is the foundation for everything.)
时间是把杀猪的刀。	*Shijian Shi Ba Sha Zhu De Dao.* (Time is like a knife that kills pigs, slow but cruel.)

LANDMARKS

胡同	*Hu Tong* (Narrow valleys that can be found in historic districts in Beijing)
昆明湖	*Kun Ming Hu* (A tranquil lake that sits at the center of the grounds of the Summer Palace in Beijing)
牛街	*Niu Jie* (A street packed with restaurants that serve traditional Beijing food and snacks—a true heaven for foodies)
四合院	*Si He Yuan* (An architectural style indigenous to Beijing; it's a common residence compound with a courtyard in the middle)
颐和园	*Yi He Yuan* (The Summer Palace, a majestic imperial garden in Beijing, beloved by the locals and beyond)

APPENDIX

—

Author's Notes

American Psychological Association. "Marriage and Divorce."
Accessed October 4, 2020. https://www.apa.org/topics/divorce.

Edmond, Charlotte. "Global Migration, by the Numbers: Who
Migrates, Where They Go and Why." World Economic Forum.
January 10, 2020. https://www.weforum.org/agenda/2020/01/
iom-global-migration-report-international-migrants-2020/.

United Lawyers (blog). "Divorce Rate by Country: The World's
10 Most and Least Divorced Nations." September 29, 2017.
Accessed October 8, 2020.

Chapter 8

Ettachfini, Leila. "What Is Birthright and Why Is It So Controversial?" *Vice,* August 15, 2019. https://www.vice.com/en/article/
j5yqd8/what-is-birthright-israel-why-controversial.

Chapter 11

Laozi. *Tao Te Ching.* Translated by Gia-fu Feng and Jane English.
New York: Vintage Books, 1972.

Chapter 13

Manet, Edouard. The Grand Canal of Venice (Blue Venice). 1875. Oil on canvas, 54 x 65 cm. Shelburne Museum, Shelburne. https://www.wikiart.org/en/edouard-manet/the-grand-canal-of-venice-blue-venice-1874.

Chapter 30

Islander Villa Escapes. "Hiking St. Lucia Pitons." Accessed October 6, 2020. https://www.islandervillas.com/st-lucia-pitons-hike.html.